Easy Family History, 2nd edition

Easy Family History, 2nd edition

The Beginner's Guide to Researching Your Family History

David Annal

BLOOMSBURY
LONDON • NEW DELHI • NEW YORK • SYDNEY

First edition published by The National Archives, Kew London in 2005.

This second edition first published in 2012 by

Bloomsbury Publishing Plc
50 Bedford Square
London WC1B 3DP
www.bloomsbury.com

A CIP record for this book is available from the British Library.

ISBN: 978-1-4081-7570-5

This book is produced using paper that is made from wood grown in
managed, sustainable forests. It is natural, renewable and recyclable.
The logging and manufacturing processes conform to the environmental
regulations of the country of origin.

Design by Fiona Pike, Pike Design, Winchester
Typeset by Saxon Graphics Ltd, Derby
Printed and bound by CPI Group (UK) Ltd, Croydon, CR0 4YY

Dedication

To my two wonderful daughters, Catherine and Isabel.

Contents

Picture acknowledgements

p. 6 David Annal

pp. 16, 30, 56 General Register Office (Identity and Passport Service)

p. 66 Principal Registry of the Family Division

p. 78 Shropshire Archives

p. 124 © and database right Crown Copyright and Landmark
Information Group Ltd (All rights reserved 2005)

p. 132 Internet Library of Early Journals

p. 162 www.freebmd.org.uk

Acknowledgments

Thanks to my wife, Liz, for reading through the text and correcting my spelling and grammar. Also, to all my former colleagues at The National Archives particularly those who I spent 10 happy years with at the Family Records Centre.

Introduction to the second edition:

The world turned upside down

In the eight years since the first edition of *Easy Family History* was published, the world of family history has changed almost beyond recognition. The original book included frequent references to websites but they were largely there as an afterthought – the emphasis was on visiting record offices and libraries to do your research with mention being made of alternative online options where they existed.

Now, of course, the situation has been turned on its head. For almost all of the major sources, the first option is to search online. It was always clear that family history research had a big online future but it is the rate of change that has surprised us all. Just over 10 years ago, when the Church of Jesus Christ of Latter-day Saints (the Mormons) broke the mould with the online launch of the International Genealogical Index (the forerunner of FamilySearch), nobody could possibly have envisaged what the online family history world would look like in 2012.

It's inevitable that these developments will continue apace, with more and more resources being digitised. But technological changes are also likely to have a significant impact on our hobby – who knows where the recent advances in the world of netbooks, tablets and other hand-held devices will lead us?

Despite all the changes in the way we access the records, the basic family history research principles remain the same – and they always will. So the second edition of this book will still focus on the key sources for family history research and look at what they can tell us about our ancestors; we'll look at how and why the records were created and we'll consider how one record source can link to another.

The title of the book was originally chosen to reflect the fact that the book covered sources which were, relatively speaking, easily accessible to most UK-based researchers. Now, as more and more material has become available online, the range of sources which fall into the category of 'easy' has widened. Perhaps the most important group of documents which can now be described as 'easy' are the records of our military ancestors; the vast collections of files and registers recording their service in the British Army, the Royal Navy, the Royal Marines and, more recently, the Royal Air Force. This second edition includes a brand-new chapter dedicated to these fascinating and informative records.

The section on emigration and immigration has also been expanded to include the wealth of material in this area now available online. It mainly covers records of British men and women leaving these shores to start new lives in America, Canada and Australia, but the global nature of research in the 21st century means that we also now have access to documents recording movement to and from many other parts of the world.

Accessing the records may be easy but tracking down our ancestors in them is rarely so. Family history research can be a serious challenge – and that's the way we like it. If it was too easy, if we really could just type a name into a website and bring up our entire family history, our research wouldn't be the enjoyable and challenging hobby that it is.

This book covers only the most important sources for family history research and these represent just the tip of a vast iceberg. If you're successful in navigating your way through the records covered here, you'll find that you're just at the start of what will almost certainly be a long and enjoyable journey.

Introduction to the first edition: Who are we? Who were they?

This book comes with an important health warning: before you start to take an active interest in your family history you should be aware that there may be no going back!

You'll soon find out that researching your family history can be highly addictive. Over the past few years this once-peaceful little hobby of ours has started to become a bit of a national obsession: articles have appeared in the national press; online releases of historical documents have brought down websites; pressure groups have been formed; and questions have even been asked in the House of Commons.

There are a number of theories as to why this outwardly bookish and academic pursuit should have caught the nation's imagination in such an extraordinary way, but the truth of the matter is that no one really knows the answer. Some look for sociological or political reasons – a growing detachment from our ancestral roots leading to a need to rediscover an idyllic past. Some put it down more simply to a natural human inquisitiveness, while others point to the growth in leisure time and the opportunities brought about by the advent of the Internet and the World Wide Web.

I'm sure that there's some truth in all of these theories and also that the answer is a combination of certain aspects of each. The role of television in all this shouldn't be underestimated: in 1979, the BBC broadcast a landmark programme called, quite simply, *Family History*. Although it was essentially a personal journey (undertaken by the broadcaster Gordon Honeycombe), it struck a chord with millions of viewers and inspired a generation of family historians.

The programme was groundbreaking in the way that it showed how 'ordinary' people could research documents recording the lives of their 'ordinary' ancestors to tell the story of their family. For the first time, family history was presented as a hobby that everyone could get involved in rather than being the exclusive preserve of the aristocracy.

Moving rapidly forward some 25 years, we come to another groundbreaking television series. In October 2004, the BBC began a series of programmes following the personal journeys of 10 celebrities as they set about discovering the truth about their ancestors. The public reaction to *Who Do You Think You Are?* took even the BBC by surprise as viewing figures topped five million for some of the shows – surpassing all other programmes broadcast on BBC2 that year.

Despite the great distance in time between the two series, they had several features in common. Neither Gordon Honeycombe nor any of the celebrities featured in *Who Do You Think You Are?* had any noble or titled ancestry; most came from 'normal' middle-class or working-class backgrounds. As well as telling some fascinating and moving stories, often tinged with a degree of sadness, both programmes took time to illustrate the actual process of family history research and to demonstrate how easy it was for people to set out on their own voyages of discovery.

And that's what this book aims to do. Each chapter covers a different source, looking at the background to the records, what information they contain and how to get the most out of them. On the way, we'll look at some of the problems you might encounter and suggest ways that you can work around them.

This book starts by looking at what most researchers would agree are the most important basic sources for family historians – birth, marriage and death certificates, census returns, wills and parish registers – and then goes on to look at some other resources that are fairly easily accessible and can provide you with additional vital information about your ancestors and the way they lived their lives.

There's an attempt to concentrate on sources that can be accessed from all parts of the country – not just London and the South East – although it's an unavoidable fact that many of the most important documents are held by The National Archives in Kew, and can only be seen there or at the Family Records Centre in London[1]. But the family history centres run by the Church of Jesus Christ of Latter-day Saints, the national network of county record offices and local studies libraries and, above all else, the Internet, have all helped to bring many of the most basic sources within easy reach of the vast majority of the population.

The book is unashamedly biased towards 19th-century sources since this is the period where you are likely to experience the greatest success in your research. The main focus is on the records of English and Welsh ancestors, but the majority of research techniques we'll examine are equally valid for other parts of the UK.

One very important skill that all newcomers to the mysterious world of family history should try to develop is the ability to read documents with a critical eye. You need to be able to look at them and understand not just what they say, but also what this information means to your research. Although you may well consider the discovery of your great-great-grandmother's birth certificate to be a fantastic achievement and a significant milestone, what is significant is not the certificate itself or the information it contains – rather, the clues that you now have to lead you on to other sources in your constant quest to uncover more and more ancestors.

But this book will also attempt to encourage you to look beyond the potentially dreary process of simply collecting names and dates for

---

1 The Family Records Centre closed in March 2008.

your family tree and to try to find out what life was really like for your ancestors. We'll look at a number of less well-known sources that will help you to do this.

Problem-solving is another important skill for family historians to develop. The ability to look at a problem in an objective way and to reach logical conclusions based on the evidence available to you comes in very handy. And when you feel that you've hit a brick wall, why not take a step back and see if you can work your way around it instead of trying to knock it down?

Family history is changing: the online revolution has probably affected our hobby more than any other leisure pursuit, and to reflect this a whole chapter has been dedicated to the Internet.

Although it is still possible to research your family history without ever setting foot in cyberspace, the number of people who are resistant to this new technology is diminishing daily. In fact, family historians are at the forefront of the Silver Surfers movement, and you might be surprised to learn how many people aged over 80 have not only come to terms with computers but are now actively spreading the word among their contemporaries.

This book attempts to get you started. It cannot, of course, cover everything: once you start to think about it, almost any document that includes a person's name could constitute a family history source; but you do have to draw the line somewhere!

One final point: throughout this book the term 'family history' has been used in preference to 'genealogy'. This is entirely a personal preference, but it's important to me. Family history is 'exactly what it says on the tin' – the history of people's families. Genealogy sounds too much like a science, too much like homework.

Family history is an enjoyable, challenging, sometimes frustrating, but ultimately rewarding hobby. Yes, you should take your research seriously, you should organise your notes efficiently and keep your files and family trees up to date, but at the same time you should keep it all in perspective. It is just a hobby – you don't have to do it and you can stop whenever you want to! But for many thousands of people, researching their family history has become a lifetime's work; and once you take that first step on your voyage of discovery, there may be no looking back.

The Davidson Family, ancestors of the author, photographed about 1905 in Edinburgh.

Chapter 1

Homework:
Your own resources

Family history begins at home
History in the attic
Family treasures
Enter, the relatives
Checklist: Interviews
Table: Key dates for family historians

Family history begins at home

It's amazing how much you can find out about your ancestors before
you even set foot in a library or a record office. You probably have lots
of sources in your own home that you've never thought of as historical
documents, and you almost certainly have a lot of basic information
about your ancestors tucked away in that remarkable archive know as
the human brain. And don't forget about your Auntie Margaret – she
knows a lot more about your ancestors than you'd think, and she's
probably been trying to talk to you about them for the past 20 years,
but you haven't been listening, have you? Well, now's the time to start.

But it's not just the memories of your relatives that will help you get
up and running – there's also the wealth of paper records that a family
naturally accumulates over the years to consider. And this is where it
pays to have relatives who possessed the 'hoarding' gene. The ancestor
who decided to deal with their deceased parents' belongings by
reducing them to cinders on a bonfire is the curse of the modern
family historian. And most families will know about the old family
photo album which Granny used to have, but no one's quite sure
where it is now.

History in the attic

There's a good chance you'll find that somewhere, someone in the family has got a little box in an attic with a collection of family papers. It probably won't be a large tea chest stuffed full of old legal documents recording the purchase of the house (that you still live in!) by your great-great-grandfather 150 years ago. Very few of us will find a diary kept by our suffragette great-grandmother, and you probably won't come across a bundle of letters written by your great-uncle to his mother from his rat-infested First World War trench. But what you do find will prove invaluable as you set out on the trail of your ancestors.

The items you're most likely to find are copies of birth, marriage and death certificates, newspaper cuttings and perhaps an old will. You might find an ancestor's employment records, trade union or club membership cards, school reports and, if you're very lucky, that holy grail of family historians, the Family Bible.

Some of these documents will be over a hundred years old and they may be in pretty poor condition. You would be well advised to get them photocopied or digitally scanned as soon as possible. Don't carry the originals around with you when you go to see relatives or visit a record office – if you do, you'll find that old paper can disintegrate rapidly and you run the very real risk of losing valuable information. These are precious documents and they are irreplaceable.

And what makes them particularly important for family historians is that you know right from the start that they relate to your ancestors. As you progress with your research you'll find that proving whether a particular birth certificate relates to your ancestor or not can be one of the most difficult tasks facing you. These documents from your attic have what we might call built-in provenance. We know where they came from and we can therefore be virtually certain that they are the very documents obtained and used by your own direct ancestors.

It's worth spending some time looking at these documents, thinking about why your ancestors might have kept them and reading them thoroughly for clues. Make notes about what they tell you about your family and, once you've added this to your personal knowledge, you should have enough information to enable you to draw up your first family tree. There's no right or wrong way to do this – a simple hand-drawn sketch on a piece of rough paper might work as well for you as one of the commercially available family tree software packages. The important thing is to record the details in a way that makes it easy for you to tell at a glance what you know about the various members of your family. And you'll probably be surprised to see how much information you already have.

Most people have some basic knowledge of their grandparents, aunts, uncles and cousins, and if you've been lucky with your box in the attic you might have a tree going back three or four generations – maybe even more. But it doesn't matter if you don't have vast amounts of family information at home – just knowing when and where you were born is enough to get you started.

Family treasures

Our Victorian and Edwardian ancestors were very keen to leave their mark on history and you may be fortunate enough to have inherited the old Family Bible, where you will find the names and dates of birth (or christening) of several generations of your family recorded. A brief note of caution here: entries in Family Bibles were often made many years after the event and therefore the dates of birth, like so many other 'facts' you'll come across while researching your family history, will need to be checked against official sources. Nevertheless, old Family Bibles really are a treasure chest, and if you don't have one yourself it's quite possible that a distant cousin may be the lucky owner.

Photographs are another great source for family historians, but frustratingly they are rarely labelled, so you may end up with a wonderful collection of pictures of your late-Victorian and Edwardian ancestors with no way of knowing whether the old gentleman with the handlebar moustache is Great Uncle Bill or his cousin Harry. However, older members of the family may be able to help you put names to some of the faces, and details such as the photographer's name and address may help you to date the image or give you a useful clue as to which branch of the family the stern old lady in the sombre black dress belonged to.

Enter, the relatives

And now's the time to start getting in touch with your cousins, uncles and aunts – anyone who's related to you who might know something about the family. The ideal candidate is the great-aunt in Tunbridge Wells who still lives in the house where your grandfather was born and knows all the old family stories. But beware: the relatives you get in touch with might not have any interest in family history whatsoever and they may not be too keen on talking about the past. They may even know something about the family that they don't want to share with you – an illegitimate birth or a criminal ancestor, or perhaps some event which reminds them of a time of sadness, like the death of a young child. So it's important to approach relatives in the right way and to treat them with respect and kindness. Also, it's a good idea to share your findings with your relatives right from the start. An old newspaper cutting could be the trigger that releases a whole flood of memories; a photo they haven't seen for years might remind them of an uncle who emigrated to Australia half a century ago, while a copy of their grandfather's birth certificate might reveal something they didn't know before. The more you involve your relatives in your research, the more likely you are to benefit from their collective reminiscences.

Don't expect your elderly relatives to know everything about the family – most of all, don't expect them to know the precise dates of family events which took place half a century ago. A question like 'When did Uncle Stan die?' is unlikely to produce results, but if you were to ask whether Stan died before or after his brother Alf, you may just get a meaningful answer. People often associate family events with national ones, so they may remember that their great-grandfather died a few days after Queen Alexandra, without knowing exactly when that was. One of the most important things to bear in mind when dealing with family stories is that they tend to get twisted – even over a fairly short period of time. We've probably all been at family gatherings where memories are being shared by distant cousins and you can almost guarantee that there will be a dispute about some detail, such as which great-uncle it was who died in the battle of the Somme or whether Cousin Alice moved to Perth or Melbourne.

It's obvious how these stories can become corrupted over hundreds of years, and while there may be a grain of truth at the root of the story (and there nearly always is), it's your job as a researcher to question it and to maintain a healthy degree of cynicism. For example, was your great-great-grandfather really a solicitor or was he in fact a solicitor's clerk? Did your ancestor really fight at the Battle of Trafalgar or did he join the crew of the Victory five years later? And did that great-uncle actually die in the Somme? Could the story that's been passed down to you be an example of an understandable exaggeration on the part of his descendants? After all, don't we all want to think the best of our ancestors, and isn't it nice to believe that they took part in some of the greatest events in history?

Once you've gathered together all the information you can find at home and you've made contact with some aunts, uncles and cousins, it's time to start looking further afield. Later in this book we will look in some detail at the vast range of family history resources now available online. It is still possible to research your family history without using the Internet but to do so would be to take an odd approach to the subject! The World Wide Web is a truly remarkable resource for family historians and a working familiarity with the major websites, both commercial and free to use, will undoubtedly make your research more rewarding. The first family history websites tended to fall into one of two categories: personal sites on which enthusiastic amateur family historians posted the results of their research, together with family photos and stories; or 'official' sites, which contained indexes to records such as census returns, wills, or births, marriages and deaths. While many of these were extremely valuable and opened up whole new avenues of research, they were still no substitute for getting access to the primary source material – the original documents that they referred to.

Today, however, all of this has changed. You will almost certainly want to take out a subscription to one or more of the major commercial sites which provide access to most (but by no means all) of the key UK family history sources, the most significant being the 1841–1911 census returns for England and Wales, vast collections of parish registers, immigration and military service records, and millions of wills dating back to the 14th century. And if you're lucky enough to have Scottish forebears you can view digital copies of thousands of family records on one dedicated official website.

The Internet is also home to a vast number of mailing lists and message boards, and this has allowed family history to become a truly worldwide pursuit. It's now relatively easy to get in touch with distant cousins not just in the US, Australia, Canada and New Zealand but also in other countries where British emigrants ended up, like Argentina, South Africa or Israel. Posting a message asking for information or offering to share information about your ancestors can produce amazing results – you never know who might read it. Simply typing a name into a good Internet search engine can throw up some interesting leads, and if you're feeling really adventurous you might even think about publishing the results of your own research online.

The last thing to mention here about the Internet is that the archives and record offices that you'll use in the course of your research all have highly informative websites which will tell you everything you need to know about planning a visit. Most of them also have online catalogues so you can check that what you want to look at is available and possibly even order it in advance. Many record offices have created online indexes to some of their most widely-used records which could give you a head start or may even save you a visit.

A list of useful websites can be found at the end of this book (see page 179).

DID YOU KNOW?

Most counties have at least one family history society – it's well worth joining your local society, as well as the ones that cover the areas that your ancestors came from. You'll get copies of journals and you can go to regular meetings where you can hear talks by experts, buy books and CDs relating to local sources and share your experiences with other researchers.

Checklist: Interviews

Ten tips for interviewing elderly relatives

· Get in touch before you visit – don't turn up announced.
· Explain what you're doing and why you're doing it.
· Take copies of relevant documents and photos with you.
· Take notes of what your relatives say.
· Share your findings.
· Don't bombard them with too many questions.
· Don't behave like an interrogator.
· Be sensitive – there may be things they don't want to talk about.
· Don't expect precise information.
· Don't believe everything they say.

Key dates for family historians (for England and Wales)

1538	Introduction of parish registers
1598	Bishops' transcripts – copies of parish registers sent to the bishops
1649–60	The Commonwealth period – gaps in parish registers
1732	All parish registers written in English rather than Latin
1752	Gregorian calendar adopted
1754	Hardwicke's Marriage Act implemented, standardising the method of recording marriages
1801	First national census taken
1813	Rose's Parochial Register Act implemented, standardising the method of recording baptisms and burials
1837	Start of civil registration of births, marriages and deaths
1841	Earliest surviving national census returns
1858	Establishment of civil probate system
1875	Registration Act passed, tightening up certain aspects of the civil registration system
1882	Married Women's Property Act implemented – married women could now legally own property
1911	Latest available census returns

Easy does it

It's understandable that when you set out on your research you will want to make as much progress as possible, as quickly as you can. But there's a danger that by going too quickly you may miss important clues, and you could even end up researching the wrong family, so it's very important that you prove each link as you go. You need to be certain that the birth certificate you have found is in fact your great-grandfather's and not that of someone else of the same name who happened to be born around the same time in the same place. This is not always as easy as it sounds, but it really is worth spending some of your valuable time on making sure that you're literally on the right lines.

Although there is no right or wrong way to go about your research, it's a good idea to follow a few basic principles. And the most important of these is that you should always start with the earliest well-documented event in your family and work backwards from there. For example, if you have a copy of your grandfather's birth certificate, the next step would be to trace his parents' marriage certificate. Once you have this, you can look for *their* birth certificates, and so on. Along the way you will use a variety of other sources, such as census returns, to help you identify the correct certificates, but if you follow this basic process of moving from one generation back to an earlier one, you won't go far wrong.

There's also a temptation to make what we might call great 'leaps of faith', assuming that since your surname is Shakespeare, or Nelson, or Nightingale you are therefore related to or even descended from the famous person of that name. Or you might have found a reference on a website to a farmer living in the 17th century who happens to have your surname and comes from the same area as you. Don't be tempted to claim him as your own before you've researched the family line thoroughly. In family history, there is no substitute for serious methodical research. Of course your research should be fun; of course you should enjoy it; but, unless you continually ask yourself whether you are certain that you can prove each step of your research, you run the very real risk of researching someone else's family history.

A certified copy of the 1845 birth certificate of George Howard Darwin, son of the biologist and theorist Charles Darwin and his wife Emma.

Chapter 2

In the beginning: Birth records

Civil registration – 1837 and all that
The General Register Office indexes
Birth certificates
Changes in 1969
Searching for a birth certificate
Non-registration of births
Linking GRO certificates to census returns
Checklist: Birth certificate searches
Adoptions

Civil registration – 1837 and all that

The first documentary sources that most of us come across when we start researching our family history are our ancestors' birth, marriage and death certificates. In England and Wales, births, marriages and deaths have been registered by the state since 1 July 1837. The year 1837 is therefore one of the most important dates for family historians to remember.

This process of state registration of births, marriages and deaths is known as civil registration and, along with the census returns, the records of these events form the backbone of the research into our family history. The certificates provide the basic facts about the most important events in a person's life and, crucially, give us invaluable information about our ancestors' parents, spouses and children. Civil registration didn't begin in Scotland until 1855 and it wasn't until 1864 that comprehensive registration of births, marriages and deaths was introduced in Ireland.

In England and Wales, the country was divided up into a number of registration districts, each of which was itself divided into sub-districts. This basic structure of districts and sub-districts is still in place today, although the boundaries and the names of the districts have changed considerably in many cases.

The local registrars were responsible for registering the births and deaths that occurred in their own districts, with separate arrangements made for marriages. The relevant information about each event was entered into a register under a number of pre-printed headed columns. At the end of every three months, the registrars sent details of all the births, marriages and deaths registered in their districts to the General Register Office (GRO).

Copies of birth, marriage and death certificates can be ordered in a number of different ways:

· online via the GRO's website at: www.gro.gov.uk/gro/content/ certificates;
· by post or by phone from the General Register Office in Southport (see page 177 for their details);
· by post or in person from the various local register offices – but only for events registered in that district – and note that the GRO's index reference numbers (i.e. the volume and page number) are of no relevance to the local registrars.

Information about current fees can also be obtained from the General Register Office (www.gro.gov.uk).

The General Register Office indexes

Once the details have been received from all the registrars in England and Wales, it's then the job of the General Register Office to compile national indexes – a job which has been carried out conscientiously and (largely) efficiently since the start of civil registration in July 1837.

The original index books were removed from public access in 2008 and the GRO indexes (often misleadingly known as the St Catherine's House indexes after one of their former locations) are now only available as sets of microfiche at the following locations:

- Birmingham Central Library
- Bridgend Reference and Information Library
- City of Westminster Archives Centre
- Manchester City Library
- Newcastle City Library
- Plymouth Central Library
- The British Library

The Society of Genealogists' Library in London, the Church of Jesus Christ of Latter-day Saints' Family Search Centres and some county record offices and larger public libraries also hold incomplete sets of the indexes.

The GRO are currently planning to develop an official electronic version of the indexes but meanwhile, most researchers search for GRO certificate references via one of a number of commercial and voluntary websites. The most useful of these are:

- www.freebmd.org.uk – a free site, run by volunteers who are extracting the information from the GRO indexes and creating a searchable (but not yet complete) database;
- www.ancestry.co.uk – the UK branch of the world's biggest commercial site. A subscription provides access to fully indexed database of birth, marriage and death registrations from 1837 to 2005;
- www.findmypast.co.uk – the biggest UK-based commercial site. Access to birth, marriage and death indexes from 1837 to 2006 (marriages to 2005 only) via a subscription service;
- www.ukbmd.org.uk – a portal site, with links to over 2,000 other sites including Local BMD, which provides access to local records of births, marriages and deaths from certain parts of the country.

These websites have revolutionised the way that family historians search for records of their ancestors' births, marriages and deaths. There's little to be said in favour of spending hours trawling through sets of microfiche when you can find the information you want in a few minutes on the Internet. However, we need to bear in mind that these online indexes have been created by a manual transcription process and even the best of them are bound to contain some errors and inaccuracies. FreeBMD (www.freebmd.org.uk) is probably the best in terms of accuracy but it is the least comprehensive. It still has some way to go before it can really be said to have replaced the GRO indexes as the primary means of access to these records, but you only need to look at the sheer volume of entries (over 200 million at the time of writing) and the sophisticated ways in which the search engine enables you to interrogate the data to see why so many family historians use this remarkable website. The days of those soul-destroying 50-year searches through the printed indexes are long gone.

It really doesn't matter whether you're searching online or on microfiche – the same principles should always apply. The results of a search in one of the online indexes will provide the GRO reference (see below) of one or more potentially relevant entries. This is a very different experience to a traditional index search, which would have led you (hopefully) to finding an entry on a particular page. In order to get the most out of your online searches, it's important to understand how the original physical indexes are structured. Since most of the websites allow the user to view digital scans of the original pages, it is quite easy to become familiar with the format of the original indexes.

Most online searches are successful and instantly produce the desired results, but there will inevitably be occasions when the record you're looking for proves difficult to track down. The tips in the main sections on birth, marriage and death certificates in this book are designed to help you to work your way through the minefield of civil registration.

Until 1983, the GRO indexes were divided into quarterly volumes. So, for each year, there are four volumes listing the births, marriages or deaths registered in:

· January, February and March
· April, May and June
· July, August and September
· October, November and December

The quarters are commonly referred to by the name of the last month of the quarter, i.e. March (MAR), June (JUN), September (SEP) and December (DEC). Since 1984 there has been a single volume of indexes for each year.

It's important to bear in mind that the indexes are arranged by the date of registration rather than the date of the event itself. This isn't a major issue with marriages, which are registered on the day of the ceremony, or with deaths, which have to be registered within five days (until 1875, within eight days). However, births can be registered up to six weeks after the event, so it is not at all uncommon to find a birth listed in the 'following' quarter. For example, a child who was born towards the end of May 1867 may not have been registered until the beginning of July. In that case, the birth would be found in the index for the September quarter of 1867.

Each quarterly volume lists the names of everyone whose birth, marriage or death was registered in that quarter. The names are listed in alphabetical order, first by surname and then, within each surname, by forename. The place shown in the index is the name of the district in which the event was registered, which is not necessarily the actual place in which it occurred. Registration districts can cover quite a large area, possibly containing several different towns. For example, the registration district of Prescot in Lancashire includes the towns of Eccleston, Hale, Knowsley, Prescot, St Helens, Widnes and Windle, as well as several smaller places. A birth, marriage or death occurring in any of these places would appear in the indexes as 'Prescot'.

The reference number shown in the indexes consists of a volume and a page number, and allows the GRO to identify a particular entry. The volume number identifies a wide geographical area, and although the numbers have changed over the years they remained the same from 1852 to 1946, the period of most interest to family historians. This can be a great help to those of us without an encyclopaedic knowledge of English geography – all events registered in Cheshire, for example, will have a volume number of 8a.

It's important to remember that the websites mentioned above provide access to the GRO's indexes and not to the registered entries themselves. The details from the registers are only available in the form of a certified copy of the entry in question. In other words, you need to obtain a copy of the certificate itself.

Birth certificates

The GRO indexes give only limited information about each registered birth:

· name
· mother's maiden surname (from SEP 1911)
· registration district
· reference number (volume and page)

The basic layout of English and Welsh birth certificates and the information they contain remained the same from the first day of registration in July 1837 right up until the end of March 1969. Each certificate shows the following information:

· when and where born
· name, if any
· sex
· name and surname of father
· name, surname and maiden surname of mother
· occupation of father
· signature, description and residence of informant
· when registered and signature of registrar
· name entered after registration

In addition, at the top of the certificate, the year of registration and the names of the registration district, the sub-district and the county are recorded. Let's have a look in more detail at each of these headings.

When and where born

This column records the date and place of the child's birth. The day and month are usually written in full, followed by the year. In the case of multiple births (twins, triplets etc.) the time of birth is also given – it is important for legal purposes (for example, inheritance of property) to know which one of a pair of twins is older. So if you come across an English or Welsh birth certificate with a time of birth, it's worth checking to see if there was another child registered at the same time. However, a number of registrars, particularly in the early years of civil registration, recorded the times of births as a matter of course.

The place of birth is usually quite precise, although it may just be the name of the village or small town – again, particularly in the early years of registration. For children born in larger towns and cities you should expect to find the full address: house number, street and town.

Name, if any

This column contains the child's forename and any middle names. Note that the surname is not entered here: it is assumed that the child has the same surname as its father, or, if no father is shown, the same as its mother. Occasionally this column was left blank, indicating that the parents hadn't chosen a name for the child by the time its birth was registered. In this case, the birth would be entered in the index as 'Male' or 'Female'. Sometimes a name was added later and this would be recorded in the column headed 'Name entered after registration'. Often the reason for the absence of a name is that the child had died before being baptised. In such cases you would expect to find a corresponding 'Male' or 'Female' death registration, usually in the same quarter.

Sex

The single word 'Boy' or 'Girl' should be entered in this column, indicating the sex of the child. From 1 April 1969, the terms 'Male' and Female' are used instead.

Name and surname of father

The first name, any middle names and the surname of the father will be found here. A blank space indicates an illegitimate birth. A potential problem to watch out for is that, before 1875, the mother of an illegitimate child could have the father's name recorded on the birth certificate whether or not he was there to confirm that he was indeed the father of the child. The 1874 Births and Deaths Registration Act closed this loophole, and from then on the father of an illegitimate child had to be present at the registration in order for his name to appear on the certificate.

Name, surname and maiden surname of mother

Along with the family's address, the mother's maiden surname is probably the most useful piece of information that you'll find on a birth certificate, as it provides a link to the parents' marriage certificate. In most cases the details entered will be something like:

Mary Smith
formerly Jones

indicating that Mary's maiden surname was Jones.

Things start to get a bit more difficult if the mother had been married before. Then you might get an entry like:

Mary Smith,
late Brown
formerly Jones

which tells us that Mary was born as Mary Jones, was previously married to someone called Brown, but is now married to Mr Smith.

In the case of an illegitimate birth, whether a father's name is given or not, the unmarried mother would normally appear as Mary Jones, with no other surnames mentioned. Unless, of course, it was an illegitimate birth to a married (or previously married) woman, in which case you might need to speak to an expert to get the correct interpretation – these things can get very complicated!

You should also bear in mind that there was nothing – other than their own sense of right and wrong – to stop an unmarried couple claiming to be married when registering a birth. The information given to the registrars was taken on trust and there was no requirement to produce a marriage certificate as evidence.

Occupation of father
This column offers very little scope for misunderstanding, confusion or ambiguity; if a father is shown on the certificate, his occupation will be entered here. There may be a temptation to exaggerate his status, but in most cases, what you see is what you get.

Signature, description and residence of informant
This is a very important piece of information which is often overlooked. The informant was usually the child's mother (most working fathers wouldn't have been able to take the time off to register a birth), but

occasionally you'll find the name of a relative who lived where the child was born (an aunt or a grandparent), and from 1875 onwards anyone who was present at the birth could act as the informant. If you see the words 'the mark of ...' together with an 'X' this usually means that the informant was illiterate, but it may simply mean that they were unable to write that day – perhaps they had a sprained wrist! Nevertheless, you should pay close attention to this, as an illiterate ancestor may have been unable to check that the details they had given had been recorded accurately.

In most cases, the informant's residence will be the same as the place of birth, but sometimes a more detailed address is given. If the address in this column is completely different from the one in the 'where born' column, then you'll need to investigate the birthplace address. It may be the address of a relative – a grandparent, for example – but it could equally turn out to be a hospital or workhouse.

When registered and signature of registrar

These columns contain little of value to family historians except that the date of registration determines which quarterly index will list the birth. The registration should occur within six weeks of the date of birth, and penalties were in place for late registration. If a birth was registered late, the certificate had to be countersigned by the Superintendent Registrar.

Name entered after registration

This column is usually left blank, but in those rare cases when a child was registered before being named there is the provision to register the name up to a year after the birth. Christian names added at baptism can also be entered here.

Changes in 1969

On 1 April 1969 a completely new format was introduced for birth certificates, which is still in use today. The place of birth of both parents is now shown on all English and Welsh birth certificates – if only this information had been recorded from the start! – and the mother's occupation is usually given, but otherwise the details are essentially the same as on earlier certificates.

Searching for a birth certificate

In order to carry out an effective search for a birth certificate in the GRO indexes, you need to know a certain amount of information about the person whose birth you're looking for, and there are a number of points you need to consider, as illustrated in the checklist on pages 27–28.

Non-registration of births

In the early years there was a certain amount of resistance to the whole idea of civil registration, and we know that from the late 1830s right up to the early 1900s a small but significant percentage of events went unregistered. This was largely a problem with births, and some parts of England and Wales seem to have been affected more than others. In 1875, the responsibility for ensuring that births were registered was transferred from the registrars to the parents, but this change doesn't seem to have had any significant impact on the rate of registration. Research has shown that the number of births registered each year increased gradually throughout the 1870s (without any sign of an increase in 1875) – in fact, the number of births registered in 1875 showed a very slight fall from the previous year.

So, if your search for a birth certificate is unsuccessful it is possible that the birth was never registered, but it's far more likely that some of the 'facts' that you know about the birth are wrong. Perhaps the person was a year or two older than you had been led to believe. Their surname may have been spelt in an unexpected way or they may even have been registered under a completely different name – their mother's maiden surname, for instance. There are a number of options to consider before giving up and assuming that your ancestor's birth wasn't registered.

Linking GRO certificates to census returns

We'll deal with census returns in some detail in Chapter 4 but at this stage it's worth looking at how birth, marriage and death certificates, and census returns are related to each other. As well as being responsible for the civil registration process, the General Register Office was in charge of taking the censuses. In order to do this as efficiently as possible, the system of registration districts and sub-districts used for registering births, marriages and deaths was also used to compile the census returns. Among other things, this enabled the GRO to compare birth rates with population change in different areas.

The details that you find on your ancestors' birth and death certificates, in particular the names of the registration district and sub-district, provide a direct link to the districts and sub-districts of the census returns. The census entry for an address found on a birth certificate will always appear amongst the contemporary returns for the registration district and sub-district that are shown on the certificate.

Checklist: Birth certificate searches

Do you know their full name (including any middle names)?

· People often used a different name to the one they were born with.
· Nicknames, such as Jack or Bill, can disguise a more 'proper' name.
· A distinctive middle name can help to identify a person's birth, but people were not always consistent about using middle names – even in official documents.
· The surname could be spelt in an unexpected way – standard spelling of names is a relatively modern phenomenon.
· The birth could have been registered under the mother's maiden name if the parents weren't actually married at the time of the child's birth.

Do you know when they were born?

· What is the source of this information?
· Remember that family memories can be flawed – the day and month are more likely to be accurate than the year.
· Do you know how old they were when they married?
· Do you know how old they were when they died?
· Do you have their age from a census return?
· Do these ages 'match'?

- Remember that information from documents can be inaccurate – the more sources you've looked at, the more likely you are to be able to discern an accurate date of birth.

Do you know where they were born?

- What is the source of this information?
- Do you have their place of birth from a census return?
- Don't forget that information from documents can be inaccurate – you may find a different place of birth given in a different census year.
- Do you know which registration district covers the place where they were born? Remember that it is the registration district that will appear in the index.

Adoptions

In 1927 the General Register Office began to register adoptions. Before this date there was no legal adoption process and children could be adopted informally, without any official record being made of the event. Unless the child kept their birth surname, it can be almost impossible to trace their origins.

The Adopted Children Register contains a record of all adoptions in England and Wales since 1 January 1927. Copies of the indexes to the Register are available on microfiche at the locations listed above (see The General Register Office Indexes). Adoption certificates must be ordered from the Adoptions Section of the General Register Office in Southport.

However, you should note that there is nothing, either in the indexes or on the adoption certificates themselves, which will enable you to identify the birth certificate of the adopted child. The child's date of birth is given, but unless the child was adopted under the same name that they were given at birth this will not really help you.

The whole process of adoption is a very sensitive matter. The Adopted Children Register is not designed to meet the needs of family historians and the General Register Office are always looking at ways of restricting access to adoption records so that only those who really need to use the records are able to do so.

Piecing together a life

It's important to understand right from the start that the documents we use in researching our family history were not designed with genealogists in mind. Birth, marriage and death certificates, census returns, parish registers, wills and other legal records were created for their own distinct purposes, and we should look on it as very fortunate that they have survived and that they are available for us to consult today. The way in which these records were compiled means that they are not necessarily arranged in the best way for family historians to use, although online indexing has largely overcome this problem.

One of the main attractions of family history is the opportunity it offers ordinary people to carry out original historical research. And for the majority of the population without any academic experience, setting out on this trail of discovery can be a unique, exciting and, at times, daunting experience. This is our chance to find out about events that took place centuries ago, to solve mysteries that have lain unsolved for years on end, to investigate how our ancestors lived and how their lives were influenced by the major events of the day.

To do all this we need to start thinking like detectives. The documents that we use are not explicitly linked – the information that you find on a marriage certificate may help you to identify the record of the bride's birth, but nothing on the certificate will unequivocally identify the correct birth certificate for her. There is no 'vital record' that brings together, on one document, the details of an individual's life. So it's up to us to create our own life records – to make the links between the various sources we use in our research – and we therefore need to be able to look at the documents with a critical eye and consider what it is they're telling us about our ancestors. We need to understand how the information we find on one document will lead us to another source and how to interpret the details that the records reveal.

A certified copy of the marriage certificate of Charles Darwin and Emma Wedgwood, 29 January 1839. As here, the marriage witnesses are often relatives.

Chapter 3

Coming together: Marriage records

Marriage certificates
Searching for a marriage certificate
Checklist: Marriage certificate searches

Marriage certificates

It would be almost impossible to carry out serious family history research without using marriage certificates at some time. The information on these certificates provides a vital bridge between generations and can open up whole new areas of research. Marriage certificates can also be quite difficult to interpret and can offer a number of traps for the unwary.

The introduction of civil marriages in 1837 was one of the most contentious aspects of a surprisingly controversial Act of Parliament. At the time of the Act, the established Church of England still wielded enormous power, particularly through the role of the bishops in the House of Lords, and they were successful in overturning several of the original proposals in the Bill, including one to introduce civil ceremonies for all marriages.

There was great resistance to the whole idea of the Church losing its exclusive role in this area, and the influence of the bishops is reflected in many of the terms of the Act as it was eventually passed. For example, even though nonconformist chapels could now be licensed for marriages, it wasn't until the 1898 Authorized Persons Act was passed that ministers could perform ceremonies without a registrar having to be present – and even then, each minister had to apply to become an 'authorized person'.

Copies of marriage certificates and the indexes to them are available from the places that were mentioned in Chapter 2 (see page 18), and all of the online resources listed are equally useful in searching for marriages. But with most marriages an alternative, and potentially cheaper, source is also available. If your Victorian ancestors were married in a church or chapel, it is highly likely that the register has been deposited in the relevant county record office, where it can be consulted (usually on microfilm) for free. Of course, the problem is knowing which church they were married in (the GRO's indexes won't tell you that), and if they married in a register office the records won't have been deposited; but if you've got more time than money on your hands, this option might be worth considering.

Increasingly, Church of England marriage registers, along with the associated baptism and burial registers, are being made available online, providing a cheap and easily accessible alternative to the GRO copies, but until this becomes more widespread it's still important to fully understand the mechanisms of the GRO's indexing and registration system as far as it relates to marriages.

The GRO's indexes to marriages show the following details for each entry:

· name
· surname of spouse (from MAR 1912)
· registration district
· reference number (volume and page)

The entries for the bride and the groom will always have the same reference number, so if you know the full names of both parties you can easily cross-reference them to ensure that you've found the right marriage. The various online indexes have made this into a very simple process, instantly linking matching entries. From 1837 to 1851, the GRO's marriage registers contained four marriages on each page, so there should be eight matching entries per GRO reference, but this was reduced to two marriages (i.e. four matching entries) in 1852.

Even in the years before each index entry included the spouse's surname, both names should be listed. The basic layout of the certificates is still the same today as it was on 1 July 1837 when marriages were first registered by the General Register Office. Each certificate shows the registration district, the year and place of the marriage and the following information about the bride and the groom:

· when married
· name and surname
· age
· condition
· rank or profession
· residence at the time of marriage
· father's name and surname
· father's rank or profession

At the bottom of the form you will find the signatures of the couple, two or more witnesses and the officiating minister or registrar, as well as information about the wedding itself – the religious denomination (if any) and whether the marriage was by licence, by certificate or after banns.

Let's look at these areas in more detail:

When married
This is usually pretty straightforward. Sometimes the year isn't given here but it should always appear at the top of the form.

Name and surname
The names of both parties (usually, but not always, including any middle names) are entered here. In the case of a widow remarrying, her former married name rather than her maiden name should be given – you'll get her maiden surname from her father's name.

Age
Frustratingly, the age is often given simply as 'Of full age', meaning that the person was 21 years or over. The good news is that, although this practice was fairly common in the early years of registration, it died out long before the end of the 19th century, and you can consider yourself unfortunate if you come across it much after the 1870s.

Condition

The marital status of both parties will be recorded here. You're most likely to find the terms 'Bachelor', 'Spinster', 'Widower' and 'Widow', although you may also stumble on the occasional 'Divorcee'.

Rank or profession

The occupation of both parties is entered here, but more often than not there will be a line or a blank space where the bride's rank or profession would appear.

Residence at the time of marriage

Compared to the addresses given on birth and death certificates, the information in this section is of relatively little use to family historians. The addresses given are frequently imprecise or simply inaccurate (see below for more on this topic).

Father's name and surname

This is occasionally left blank, which would normally indicate illegitimacy, but it is not unknown for a deceased father's name to be omitted.

Father's rank or profession

Both the groom's and bride's fathers' occupations are entered here.

It's easy to see how useful marriage certificates are. They provide you a direct link from one generation to another and the ages of the bride and groom, combined with their fathers' names, can help you to identify records of their births. You can also learn about your ancestors' religious persuasion; a marriage in a Baptist chapel, for example, could lead to the discovery of a long tradition of nonconformity in the family.

However, marriage certificates can also be the most frustrating of documents to work with. The problem is that all the information supplied by the bride and groom was taken on trust by the clerk or the registrar and very rarely questioned, yet there are any number of reasons why the couple may have chosen to be 'economical with the truth'.

Of the three major life events recorded by the GRO, marriages are the only ones where you provide the information yourself: your birth is usually registered by one of your parents and your death by your next of kin, but with a marriage, you're the one supplying the details. And whereas births and deaths are registered in private, the marriage register is signed publicly in front of the minister or registrar, as well as two or more witnesses. There are also a number of restrictions regarding marriage; most notably age, marital status and relationship to a chosen partner.

All of this presents a determined couple with the temptation to tell a few half-truths, untruths or even downright lies in order to get married without too many difficult questions being asked. Technically, anyone doing so was guilty of perjury, but you'd be amazed to find out how many of our ancestors lied – and got away with it.

And it's easy to see how this can cause problems when it comes to understanding what the certificate is telling you. The first and most common problem you might encounter is with the ages of the bride and groom. People under the age of 21 needed their parents' consent in order to marry, but since there was no requirement to produce evidence of age (and it was very rarely checked by the person performing the ceremony) it was quite easy for a 19 year old to claim to be 21 or 'of full age'. An older woman marrying a younger man might knock a few years off her age, and where there was a substantial age difference between the couple there was often a tendency to 'narrow the gap'. For example a 40-year-old man marrying a woman of 25 might be recorded in the register as 35 and 30 respectively. And remember that 'of full age' doesn't mean 21 years old or even 'over 21', as some people seem to believe: it actually means '21 years old or more'. A 62 year old could as easily be described as 'of full age' as a 22 year old.

The marital condition can also present problems. At a time when divorce was not a realistic option for most ordinary people, it was simpler for a man wanting to remarry while his 'first' wife was still alive to declare himself to be either a bachelor or a widower. As long as he was marrying in an area where he wasn't known, it was unlikely that anyone would ever find out. However, bigamy was considered a very serious crime and many people were prosecuted and even imprisoned.

Addresses on marriage certificates are notoriously imprecise or even inaccurate. Marriages taking place within the Church of England had to be performed either by licence or after the calling of banns. The process of marrying by banns was by far the cheaper of the two options, but first there were a few hurdles to jump. Banns had to be called in the parish church for three successive weeks preceding the date of the ceremony, allowing people who might know of a reason why the couple were not legally allowed to marry to make an objection – there are numerous examples of the bride's father forbidding the banns on the second or third week of calling! If the couple came from two different parishes, the banns would be called in both.

The parties also had to be resident in the parish for at least a week before the banns were called. In practice, this was a difficult rule to enforce – after all, residency is not an easy thing to prove one way or another – and for this reason the address given on a marriage certificate is often no more than an address of convenience. It may have been a temporary lodging or it may have been the residence of one of the witnesses, but there's a distinct possibility that your ancestor never actually lived there. Alarm bells should certainly start to ring when you find the same address given for the bride and the groom. It is unlikely that they lived together (in the modern sense of the phrase) before getting married, although the groom may have been a lodger in the bride's house – and again, it's possible that they had both simply given an address of convenience in order to meet the residency requirements.

Another area which causes a great deal of difficulty on marriage certificates surrounds the fathers' details. There are two potential stumbling blocks here; first, there's the problem that confronts you when you come across a big blank space where the father's name should be. As mentioned before, this usually indicates that the person marrying was illegitimate, but as always with marriage certificates, it's not as simple as that. In the 19th century there was a very real stigma attached to illegitimacy. Despite the fact that a fairly sizeable percentage of the population was illegitimate, it wasn't something that was discussed openly or readily admitted to. So when an illegitimate person went to church to get married there was a strong temptation to invent a father – usually conveniently deceased.

And that brings us on to the other main area of confusion regarding the fathers' details. None of the various Marriage Acts carried an explicit instruction to indicate whether the fathers of the bride and groom were dead or alive at the time of the wedding. Some clerks did so, by entering the word 'deceased' in brackets after the father's name, but many didn't, and it's this inconsistency that can lead you to misinterpret the information that you're presented with: because the absence of the word 'deceased' does not necessarily mean that the father was still alive. The rule of thumb here is that if neither father is described as deceased you should assume in the first place (and until you find evidence to the contrary) that both are still alive. If one of the fathers is described as deceased, it's fairly safe to assume that the other one is alive, while if both are shown to be deceased they probably were – although you can't rule out wishful thinking on the part of the bride or groom. And don't forget the possibility, mentioned above, that the 'deceased' father was actually fictitious.

Fathers' occupations were often exaggerated on marriage certificates, so don't take them too literally.

As with the signatures on birth certificates, watch out for people making their marks where their signatures should be – an indication of possible illiteracy. And bear in mind that if you were unable to read and write you would also be unable to check what the clerk had written for accuracy. Two witnesses were required to testify to the accuracy of the information supplied and to confirm that there was no 'lawful impediment' preventing the couple from marrying. Although they were usually relatives or friends of the couple it's not uncommon to find that 'professional' witnesses were employed. A shilling or two would secure the services of a churchwarden if there were no relatives on hand. And remember that the GRO versions of marriage certificates do not show the actual signatures – these will only be found in the original church, chapel or register office copies.

The best advice is to use the information that you get from marriage certificates with extreme caution. It may be reliable and it may not. It's only by comparing the details with information from other sources that we can untangle the web of deceit that some of our ancestors left behind.

DID YOU KNOW?

Hardwicke's Marriage Act was passed in 1753 and came into effect the following year. This Act is particularly important for family historians. It outlawed clandestine marriages and meant that the vast majority of marriages in England and Wales between 1754 and 1837 took place in Church of England parish churches. Only Jews and Quakers were exempt from the terms of the Act.

Searching for a marriage certificate

Searching for a marriage certificate in the GRO indexes used to be a difficult process, but it has been made much easier by the advent of online indexes. One of the first things to consider is which of the two names you're going to search under. It might seem obvious to look for the less common of the two, but if the surname is very uncommon there's a chance that it has been spelt incorrectly, so you might want to try the more common name instead. It doesn't really matter which you choose as the marriage should be indexed under the names of both parties. When using the online indexes beware of possible transcription errors – this is particularly important when it comes to the GRO reference (the volume and page number) as a simple error in transcribing this data could mean that the couples getting married are not 'matched' by the system.

Checklist: Marriage certificate searches

Do you know their full names (including any middle names)?

- People often used a different name to the one they were born with.
- One or both of the surnames could be spelt in an unexpected way – standard spelling of names is a relatively modern phenomenon.

Do you know where they were married?

- What is the source of this information? Remember that family memories can be flawed!
- Do you know how old they were when they were married?
- Do you know when their first child was born?
- Marriage under the age of 17 was extremely rare – most people married in their early to mid twenties.

Do you know where they were born?

- What is the source of this information?
- Do you know where their first child was born?

- Do you know where the bride came from? A large proportion of marriages took place in the bride's 'home' parish.
- Do you know which registration district covers the place where they were married? Remember that it is the registration district that will appear in the index.

Asking the right questions

The first task you should undertake when you get hold of a new document is to ask yourself whether there can be any doubt that you have the right one. If, for example, you've just got a copy of a birth certificate which you are hoping relates to your ancestor, have a look at the father's occupation and check that it matches what you already know about him. If you were expecting a merchant banker and what you've got in your hands is a bricklayer, then it's probably not the right certificate. Of course, some people did change jobs during their lives, but a tradesman or an artisan is unlikely to become an agricultural labourer in later life and you wouldn't expect a clerk to end up working down a mine.

Only when you've proved beyond reasonable doubt that the document is 'yours' can you start planning the next stage of your research. We've already seen how important it is to question the 'facts' supplied by your relatives, and you'll soon find out that it's also your job as a family history detective to question the accuracy of the information on the documents you uncover. It's impossible to quantify the extent of the problem, but it's certainly true to say that a substantial percentage of the birth, marriage and death certificates and the censuses that you'll look at in the course of your research contain information that is, to some degree, inaccurate.

There are a number of quite separate reasons for this. First, there's the whole range of problems brought about by illiteracy and regional accents, which we'll look at in more detail in Chapter 4. You also need to bear in mind that, when you order a certificate from the General Register Office, what you're getting is a copy of a copy of the original. The registrar may have recorded the details accurately at the time the event was registered, but it's quite easy to see how mistakes can creep in when the quarterly returns are sent to the GRO. However thorough the clerk was, however meticulously he transcribed the details from the registers, he was only human and as prone to error as the rest of us.

We've already touched on the next cause of inaccuracy on our ancestors' documents, and it's probably the most significant one. Whether we like it or not, the fact of the matter is that our ancestors had all manner of reasons why they might not be entirely truthful when it came to completing census forms and registering births, marriages and deaths.

The final point to consider here is that our ancestors might simply not have known the 'truth'. A person who didn't know where they were born might have found it easier to invent a place of birth than to admit his ignorance when the census enumerator came calling.

If the information you've got is accurate then your research will be that much easier and more straightforward, but if things start not to add up, if you're failing to find your ancestors where you'd expect to find them, then you need to start asking yourself some questions. 'Could my ancestor have been lying about his age when he got married? Was he really born in Birmingham? His marriage certificate indicates that his father was called John, but could this be a mistake for Joseph?' The best way to tackle these problems is to find as many records of your ancestors as possible. Try to find them in each of the census returns to see if any of the details are different, or simply clearer. And don't forget the possibility of a second marriage and the information you could get there. Whatever else you do, keep asking the right questions!

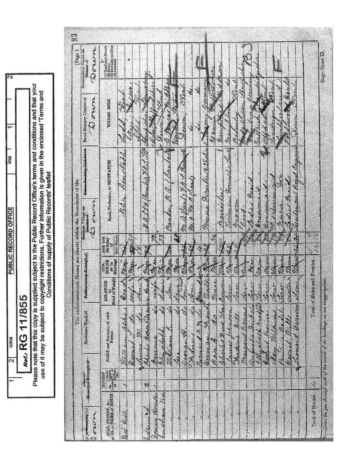

The census return for Charles Darwin's home at Downe House, Kent, 1881. Family, servants and visitors are all shown.

Chapter 4

Counting the people: Census returns

Table: The dates of the censuses
The 1841 census
The 1851 to 1901 censuses
Viewing the censuses
The 1911 census
Finding your ancestors in the census returns

The dates of the censuses

1801	Tuesday 10 March
1811	Monday 27 May
1821	Monday 28 May
1831	Sunday 29 May
1841	Sunday 6 June
1851	Sunday 30 March
1861	Sunday 7 April
1871	Sunday 2 April
1881	Sunday 3 April
1891	Sunday 5 April
1901	Sunday 31 March
1911	Sunday 2 April
1921	Sunday 19 June (available in January 2022)

In 1801 an event took place which has had an enormous impact on family historians. This was the year when the first national census was taken, and every 10 years since then (apart from in 1941, when the country was occupied with other matters) the process has been repeated.

There has always been a degree of suspicion about why the government was asking all these questions, and in order to encourage people to give the information certain guarantees were given about the confidentiality of the census returns. The result of this is that the returns are 'closed' for a hundred years and the 1911 census is therefore currently the latest available. The census forms themselves contain some of the most valuable information that family historians will ever come across – it's almost as if they were created with us in mind. But the real purpose of the censuses has always been to enable the government of the day to understand what was happening to the population and to assist with long-term planning of public services and expenditure.

The returns from the 19th century record the dramatic change in Britain from a predominantly rural society in 1801 to a heavily urbanised one a hundred years later. It's the arrangement of the censuses that makes them so useful. A schedule was delivered to each household in the week before census day (which since 1841 has always been a Sunday) and the completed forms were collected on the following Monday. The details were then copied into the census books by the enumerators. The returns for each household record the names and certain other details of every person who was present there on the night of the census – and, crucially for our purposes, they show how the various members of the household were related to each other.

However, the first censuses were simply headcounts, and it wasn't until the fifth decennial census in 1841 that the government started to ask for this detailed information about individuals. The official returns from the first four censuses were destroyed after the statistical information had been taken from them, but some of the enumerators compiled lists of the names of the people living in their districts and a small number of these lists have survived. If you're very lucky you might just find a pre-1841 census for the parish where your ancestors lived.

The 1841 census

The 1841 census is, therefore, effectively the first of the 19th-century censuses, but even this doesn't give us a huge amount of information about our ancestors. The schedules record details for each household under the following headings:

- NAMES of each person who abode therein the preceding night
- AGE and SEX:
  - Males
  - Females
- PROFESSION, TRADE, EMPLOYMENT or of INDEPENDENT MEANS:
  - Where born
  - Whether born in same county
  - Whether born in Scotland, Ireland or foreign parts

The address of each household is also given, although this is often no more than the name of the village, and house numbers are rarely shown. Middle names are not entered as a rule, but it's the age columns in 1841 which lead to the greatest confusion. The instructions to the enumerators were to round down the ages of all people aged over 15 to the nearest five years. Therefore, anyone aged between 20 and 24 should appear in the 1841 census as 20, and a 72 year old would be entered as 70. This rule wasn't always strictly applied and it's not uncommon to find the precise ages of adults, but you need to be careful with how you interpret the information in these columns.

There's not a lot of room on the forms for the occupations and they do tend to be quite vague and imprecise. They are also often heavily contracted so you should make sure that you're familiar with some of the most common abbreviations:

Ag Lab (or AL)	Agricultural labourer
MS	Male servant
FS	Female servant
Ind	Independent i.e. 'of independent means'
Ap	Apprentice
Shoe m	Shoemaker

The last two columns relate to the individual's place of birth, but the information here is unfortunately not very useful for our purposes. In the majority of cases all you get is a 'Y' (for Yes) in the column headed 'Whether Born in same County' and all this tells you is that your ancestor was born in the county in which they were then living – it's not a lot to go on and it's also frequently inaccurate. It's even more frustrating to find an 'N' in this column, as this suggests that your ancestor was born in another county but gives you no clue as to which one!

The 1851 to 1901 censuses

The questions asked in the censuses, between 1851 and 1901, are almost identical as far as the information relating to our ancestors is concerned. There was a gradual increase in the amount of detail that was requested concerning the buildings that our ancestors lived in, and new questions regarding employment status and mental and physical health were introduced over the years, but the basic structure and layout of the census page remained the same throughout the whole of this period.

At the top of the page there was a series of boxes that identified the locality. In 1851 this included the names of the parish or township, ecclesiastical district, city or borough, town and village. By the end of the century, the number of boxes had increased to eight:

· administrative county
· civil parish
· ecclesiastical parish
· county borough, municipal borough or urban district
· ward of municipal borough or urban district
· rural district
· parliamentary borough or division
· town or village or hamlet

This information shouldn't be ignored as it all helps to gain a better understanding of the sort of area that your ancestors lived in.

The rest of the census page was divided into a number of columns in which the enumerator entered the details of each household and, more importantly for us, recorded some illuminating facts about our ancestors. In each of the censuses from 1851 to 1901, the following information was recorded about each person:

· name and surname
· relation to head of family

· marital condition
· age
· profession or occupation
· where born

It's not hard to see how enormously useful this information can be, particularly when your ancestors are so conveniently packaged together in family groups. The name, age and place of birth of an individual provide you with all the information you need to carry out an effective search for their birth certificate, and if you're looking for a marriage, the age of the oldest child should help you to determine when the event is likely to have taken place.

But the censuses are no different to any other documentary evidence that our ancestors left behind and, as we've already seen with marriage certificates, there are a number of reasons why the information may be inaccurate. The very process by which the census was taken presents ample opportunity for mistakes to creep in. The high level of illiteracy in the 19th century meant that many householders were unable to complete the census schedules themselves. In these cases, the enumerator would ask the questions and note down what he heard. This could lead to all sorts of problems with unusual names – both personal names and place names – particularly if the householder had a strong regional accent which was unfamiliar to the enumerator.

Ages on census returns are frequently inaccurate and need to be treated with extreme caution – there are countless examples of people ageing substantially more, or a lot less, than 10 years between censuses! Whether this is due to the householder's ignorance, a deliberate attempt to deceive or an error by the enumerator it's difficult to say, but you should never rely on the age being accurate until you've checked it against other sources.

The 'where born' column can throw up just as many problems and can lead to the same sort of difficulties when tracing birth certificates. Something to watch out for here is that people tend to be less precise about their birthplace the further away from it they are. For example, a person born in Moseley in Staffordshire but living in London might say that they were born in Wolverhampton (the nearest large town), and if they were living in the West Midlands they might give their place of birth as Wednesfield (the parish which includes Moseley), but only if they were living in the Wednesfield area itself would they actually specify Moseley as their birthplace.

Another problem (although admittedly not a very common one) is that some people simply didn't know where they were born, and it can be very frustrating to find the letters NK (for 'not known') entered where the place of birth should be. In 1891 and 1901, census returns in Wales asked an additional question concerning the language spoken by each person: Welsh, English or both. In 1901, a similar question was asked on the Isle of Man regarding the Manx language.

DID YOU KNOW?

The first four national census returns, taken in 1801, 1811, 1821 and 1831, were simply headcounts, and no official records were made of individual names. However, some conscientious enumerators made lists of the inhabitants in their areas and a small number of these lists have survived. They are usually found in the relevant county record office.

The 1911 census

It had long been felt that the process of transcribing the details from the householders' schedules, which had been employed ever since the first full census in 1841, was both time-consuming and prone to error. The officials involved in planning the 1911 census therefore took the rather brave decision to do away with this part of the process and compile the census data directly from the householders' schedules. At the same time, it was decided to introduce a wide range of new questions and to expand the scope of several of the existing questions.

The result of this is that the 1911 census is significantly different to those that went before it. The total number of columns on the form rose from 10 to 16 with additional detail being requested regarding occupations, birthplaces and citizenship, but the biggest change was undoubtedly the whole new range of questions relating to 'fertility in marriage'.

With the earlier censuses, we only have access to the enumerators' forms, but what we're looking at here are the ones completed by our great-great-grandparents over a hundred years ago, in their own handwriting and complete with their errors, crossings out and, occasionally, their extraneous, unsolicited comments!

In addition to the individuals' details, the 1911 census forms record the total number of males and females and the number of rooms in the 'house, tenement or apartment' together with the address, as recorded by the householder. The full address is recorded on the reverse of the sheet.

The following details are recorded about each individual:

· Name and surname
· Relationship to head of family
· Age last birthday (and gender)
· Particulars as to marriage
   – Single, married, widow or widower
   – Completed years the present marriage has lasted (married women only)
   – Children born alive to present marriage (married women only)
      - Total children born alive
      - Children still living
      - Children who have died
· Personal occupation
· Industry or service with which worker is connected
· Employer, worker or working on own account
· Whether working at home
· Birthplace
· Nationality of every person born in a foreign country
· Infirmity

This is a significant amount of information to discover about our recent relatives, and as the 1911 census may well be the first documentary source we come across, the details we find here can give us an enormous head start as we set off on our quest. It's not hard to see how the additional details about our ancestors' marriages and the number of children they'd had can help to lead us on to other useful records about them.

The birthplace column is of particular interest to those of us with Scottish and Irish ancestors as, for the first time, the name of the 'County, and town or parish' of birth were to be given. In previous years the instructions were simply to write 'Scotland' or 'Ireland'.

For the 1911 census, there is also an associated set of enumerators' summary books (ESBs) in which the enumerators entered, next to each address, a description of the property (i.e. Private house, Shop, Hotel, Beer house etc.), the name of the occupier and the total number of people entered on each schedule. The summary books also provide a physical description of the district, including the various administrative units (Civil and Ecclesiastical Parish, Borough, Ward, Rural or Urban District, and Parliamentary Division), along with useful statistical information and the signatures of the census officials.

DID YOU KNOW?

From 1851 onwards, the census was taken either at the end of March or at the beginning of April. It's important to know this when you're trying to calculate your ancestors' dates of birth. If someone's age was given as seven at the time of the 1861 census, don't assume that they were born in 1854 – in fact, they would have been born sometime between April 1853 and March 1854.

Viewing the censuses

The census returns for the whole of England and Wales (including the Channel Islands and the Isle of Man) for each of the census years from 1841 to 1911 are accessible on a number of commercial websites, including Ancestry and FindMyPast. The advent of these indexed online databases, with search results linked to digital images of the original census pages, has seen a fundamental change in the way that family historians use census returns. What was once a slow, laborious process involving painstaking, lengthy, often fruitless searches through reels of microfilm, has become a relatively simple matter of entering details in an online search engine. And the benefits of being able to find each of your ancestors in every census year are enormous.

There are still occasions when you might want to browse through the returns for a particular place or find the entry for a specified address and, although this is not as easy to do as it once was, it's still possible. The various websites each allow some degree of browsing but The National Archives in Kew holds a complete set of census returns on microfilm. The microfilms have to be ordered as if they were original documents. Local and county record offices usually hold the returns for their own areas of interest (again on microfilm), and the Church of Jesus Christ of Latter-day Saints' worldwide network of family history centres can give you access to the returns for any area, although the microfilms will need to be ordered (for a small fee).

Finding your ancestors in the census returns

You should always attempt to find your ancestors in each of the censuses – partly to 'iron out' any problems with ages and places of birth, but also because you just never know what will turn up. The elderly aunt staying with the family, the distant cousin from Cornwall or the previously unknown child who must have died young can all add to the story of your family and could even open up new areas for further research.

Nowadays, finding your ancestors, wherever they were living, shouldn't prove too difficult. However, as with all online databases, you need to be aware of the usual concerns about accuracy and completeness: searching for ancestors in the census is not always as straightforward as the websites would like you to believe.

The ability to successfully interrogate any of the online family history databases is a skill which all serious modern family historians have to develop. Sometimes simply entering your ancestor's name, together with one or two supporting pieces of information, such as an approximate age or their place of birth, will produce the desired results. But what if the search is unsuccessful? What do you then?

The temptation for the inexperienced researcher is to assume that the person you're looking for is missing from the census but this is almost certainly not the case. The process behind the taking of censuses ensured that virtually everyone was 'captured' and, with the exception of the 1861 census (where approximately 3 per cent of the returns are known to be missing) and some isolated sections from 1841, 1851 and 1871, the 19th and early 20th century censuses for England and Wales are effectively comprehensive.

If your initial search fails to turn your ancestor up, you need to adapt your search. Broaden the age range or enter the name of the county instead of the parish in the birthplace field; think about how using 'wildcards' might help; try leaving some of the data out of your search to produce more results. The piece of data which is most likely to have been mistranscribed is the surname. You'll be amazed at how often the simple strategy of leaving the surname out of your search and entering a combination of first name, age and birthplace will turn up trumps.

Checklist: Online census searches

Less is more

- Enter as few details as possible.
- Try different combinations of name, age and birthplace.
- Try using just the first name or just the surname.
- Search using just the parish of residence.

Use wildcards

- * stands for any number of characters (including no characters).
- ? stands for a single character.

Avoid precise birthplaces where possible

- People were not always consistent when it came to giving their birthplace.
- As a rule, people tend to be less precise the further they are from their place of birth.

Consider alternative spellings

- Standardised spelling of personal names and place names is a relatively modern concept.
- Where names have been mistranscribed, thinking about the written 'shape' of the name is often more likely to produce results than considering variant spellings.

- The mistake is just as likely to have been made by the original enumerator as by a modern transcriber.

Where possible, search for children rather than adults

- Children's ages are more likely to be accurately recorded.

Search for the family member with the least common first name

- Search for Herbert Smith, rather than his brother John.
- Be aware that less common names are more likely to have been mistranscribed.

The name game

In Charles Dickens's classic novel *Great Expectations*, Pip, the hero of the story, asks his brother-in-law Joe Gargery how he spells his surname, to which Joe replies, 'I don't spell it at all'. This exchange tells us all we need to know about standards of literacy in Victorian England. The fact of the matter is that the vast majority of the population couldn't read or write, and it wasn't until the Education Act of 1870 that the situation began to change and a degree of basic literacy became the norm.

Until then, the spelling of surnames and place names on census returns, GRO certificates and other documents we use, was only really of importance to the clerks who wrote the documents. If there's one lesson you should learn about family history research, it is to throw away the idea of a 'correct' way to spell your name. Names can and do get corrupted and altered over the years – take the surname Shakespeare for example. Here are just a few variations you might come across:

SHAKESPEAR   SHAXSPERE   SHAKESPIEAR
SHAKYSPERE   SHAKSPEARE   SHAKESPURRE
SHACKSPERE

And none of these is any more 'correct' than any of the others. There is no right or wrong – they are simply examples of how a clerk might interpret what he heard. And this can become even more complicated when you throw regional accents into the mix. Take the case of your illiterate ancestor moving from Yorkshire to London and then being called upon to register the birth of his child. You can imagine how easy it would be for the registrar to get one or two details wrong.

Or consider the family that moved from Somerset to Durham and, when it came to census time, told the enumerator that they were born in Crewkerne. You can easily forgive the enumerator for writing down Crooken in his book!

Another common error to look out for is the dropped 'H' at the start of the name – Horwood can easily become Orwood – and the other side of the coin is that you may find that an over-zealous clerk has added an 'H', wrongly assuming that one had been dropped. It's important to keep an open mind here and make sure that you stop yourself from saying 'But that's not how my name is spelt!'

Remember that the whole concept of standard spellings of names is a relatively modern phenomenon. You should think carefully about how your surname might have been spelt in the past. Even very common names like Smith and Brown can be prone to different spellings (Smyth, Smithe, Browne, Broun etc.) and the more uncommon your name is, the greater the chance that it has experienced a variety of spellings over the centuries.

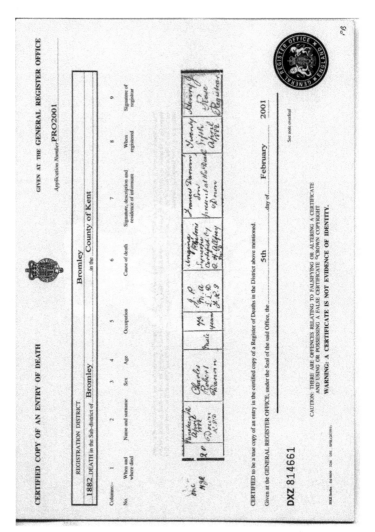

A certified copy of the death certificate of Charles Darwin, 19 April 1882. Cause of death: 'angina'.

Chapter 5

Ashes to ashes:
Death records

Death certificates
Searching for a death certificate
Checklist: Death certificate searches

Death certificates

Death certificates are often overlooked as a source for family historians, or at best they are undervalued. It's true to say that there is less information on a death certificate of an obviously genealogical nature than you would expect to find on birth or marriage certificates, but they certainly shouldn't be ignored.

Tracing records of deaths can be a frustrating and sometimes quite difficult process – particularly as the GRO's indexes didn't include ages until 1866. Before then, they showed only the following information:

· name
· registration district
· reference number (volume and page)

So if the person you're looking for had a name that was at all common, you might have real problems finding their death in this period. The deceased person's age is shown from 1866 until 1969, from which year their date of birth is shown instead. The layout of English and Welsh death certificates was the same from the start of registration in 1837 until March 1969. As with the birth certificates of the same period, the details were entered into a number of headed columns:

- when and where died
- name and surname
- sex
- age
- occupation
- cause of death
- signature, description and residence of informant
- when registered
- signature of registrar

Again, we need to have a look at each of these headings in more detail.

When and where died
The place of death will normally be the deceased person's home address, but many people died in workhouses or hospitals some distance from where they lived. Crucially for our purposes, these institutions may have been situated in a completely different registration district, and since deaths are always registered in the district in which they occur this might complicate the search for your ancestor's death. This is mainly a problem in London, with its physically small but densely populated registration districts, but even in rural areas it's a problem that you might occasionally come up against. And don't overlook the possibility that your ancestor may have died suddenly, either at work or while travelling.

Name and surname
Married women and widows will be listed under their married names i.e. their husband's surname. If they had been married more than once, only the latest surname will be shown.

Sex
The single word 'Male' or 'Female' should be entered here.

Age
The information here is normally pretty reliable, but bear in mind that the informant (see below) may not have known the deceased very well. Also remember to always consider the not uncommon phenomenon of 'rounding up' ages to the nearest 10 with older people.

Occupation

This is a rather misleading heading and the information recorded here is not always what you might expect. If the deceased was an adult male then his occupation will be entered, but if the deceased was a woman or a child then it can start to get quite complicated.

Children will normally be described as the 'son of ...' or the 'daughter of ...' and married or widowed women as the 'wife of ...' or the 'widow of ...' followed in each case by the name of their father or husband and his occupation. The situation with unmarried women is even more confusing and you may come across any one of a number of possibilities. An occupation might be given, but more often than not you'll find the words 'daughter of ...' together with the father's name and occupation. There could even be a blank space or a line through the box. An interesting example of the rather confused thinking behind all this is the case of Florence Nightingale, who died in 1910 at the age of 90. Her death certificate describes her as the daughter of William Edward Nightingale – a man who had died some 36 years previously. There's a very strong case here for arguing that Florence could perhaps have been credited with having an occupation of her own!

Cause of death

There are a couple of problems you might encounter here. First, before the implementation of the 1874 Registration Act (which tightened up and clarified several aspects of the original Birth and Deaths Registration Act of 1836), the cause of death has a tendency to be rather vague. Entries such as 'Old age' or 'Senile debility' are not at all uncommon, and when you come across 'Visitation from God' as a cause of death you do begin to wonder about the accuracy of the other details on the certificate.

Secondly, from 1875 death registrations had to be certified by a doctor, and from this point on a good dictionary will come in handy for interpreting the causes of death, which are normally given in their full medical form. Many of the diseases will be well known to us, such as cholera, typhus and bronchitis, but you may not have come across terms like 'syncope' (a faint caused by the heart stopping beating, which could often result in death) and 'phthisis' (more familiar to us as consumption or tuberculosis, that frequent killer of young Victorian women). The causes of death of our working-class urban ancestors can make for quite upsetting reading, but it all helps us to build up a better picture of the conditions they had to endure – and discovering these distressing aspects of their lives (and deaths) is just as important as learning about the good times.

Signature, description and residence of informant
This may seem obvious, but the person whose death is being registered did not provide the details to the registrar! And the identity of the person who did provide the information is therefore quite crucial to us, as the reliability and accuracy of the information on the certificate is entirely dependent on how well that person knew the deceased. So, if the informant was the person's spouse, there's every reason to believe that the details are accurate; but if a neighbour performed the task you may want to examine the details with a more critical eye.

When registered
From 1837 until 1874 deaths had to be registered within eight days of the event. This was then reduced to five days under the terms of the 1874 Registration Act. In practice, most deaths were registered within two or three days. Where an inquest had taken place, particularly if the death was of a suspicious nature, the registration could be delayed considerably. And remember that it's the date of registration which determines when the death will be entered in the GRO's indexes. Although the vast majority of deaths are registered in the same quarter as they occurred, you should never ignore the possibility that the entry will be found in the quarter following the date of death.

Signature of registrar
Unless your ancestor was a registrar, this is unlikely to be of any significance to you!

Additional information
From 1 April 1969 the deceased person's date and place of birth are shown on death certificates. Also from this date, the maiden surname of married or widowed women is recorded.

It's a good idea to get copies of as many death certificates as possible – at least for your direct ancestors – simply because you just don't know what you will find. Death certificates provide you with links to so many other sources (for example wills, newspaper reports and burial or cemetery records) and if you're fortunate enough to discover an ancestor who died suddenly under mysterious or perhaps even grisly circumstances, then you could be in for a treat!

The clue here will be a reference to an inquest and, although it is probable that the actual record of the proceedings won't have survived, the chances are that there will have been a report in the local newspaper. Be warned that these reports can be quite graphic – there was nothing our Victorian ancestors liked more than reading about gruesome, horrific deaths at the breakfast table. And if there is a report, you are likely to get some invaluable biographical details that paint a picture of your ancestors and their daily lives which you simply won't be able to get from the usual official documents.

DID YOU KNOW?

As part of her campaign to raise awareness of the effects of poor housing and unsanitary living conditions on the health of the population, Florence Nightingale asked the GRO to include questions on the 1861 census that would provide her with statistical data. In a letter to William Farr she wrote, 'We should have a return of the whole sick and diseases in the UK for one spring day which would give a good average idea of the sanitary state of all classes of the population.' Her request was not met.

Searching for a death certificate

One of the most difficult aspects of finding the record of a death is to know where to start searching. With a birth or a marriage you can use ages and children's details from census returns to work out when the events were likely to have taken place, while the best you can hope for with a death is to use the 'disappearance' of a family member between one census and the next to narrow the search down to ten years at the most.

The only alternative is to start with the last date when you know for certain that your ancestor was alive and begin your search from there. By using an online database such as FreeBMD, most searches for death certificates are now quite straightforward, but if the name is at all common, identifying the correct entry can still be fraught with difficulties.

Another approach to the problem might be to see if your ancestor left a will. Knowing when their will was proved should lead you to a record of their death. We'll have a closer look at wills in the next chapter.

Checklist: Death certificate searches

Do you know their full name (including any middle names)?

· A person's death could be registered under a different name to the one by which they were commonly known.
· Married women and widows will be registered under their married name.

Do you know when they died?

· What is the source of this information?
· Details taken from tombstones can be inaccurate, as they were often engraved many years after the event.
· Remember that dates provided by relatives may be no more than guesswork.

Do you know where they died?

· What is the source of this information?
· If someone died while they were away from home, their death would be registered in that place rather than their usual place of residence.
· Older people often moved to be close to their relatives.

Do you know how old they were when they died?

· What is the source of this information?
· Remember that ages from sources such as marriage certificates and census returns, and even the age recorded at death, can be inaccurate.

Get organised

Even if you decide at first to concentrate all your efforts on just one of your ancestral lines, you'll soon find that the amount of information you've gathered begins to get out of hand. Those hastily scribbled notes you made on the back of an envelope during the phone call to Uncle Harold, that list of birth references you noted down when you were searching online last night and the family group you found in the 1881 census are all vital pieces of evidence. But can you honestly say that you really have all the facts at your fingertips? Is the information organised in a way that makes it easily accessible? You may not even realise that you have a problem until you're contacted by a distant cousin in Canada and you try to put together a clear and concise reply to her email, summarising what you know about your bit of the family.

So you need to give careful consideration to how you are going to organise the results of your research. And there's no right or wrong way to go about it. Some people are quite happy to use paper systems, printing out references found online and typing up the results of visits to record offices, while others store all of their information electronically. Nowadays many researchers use one of the numerous software packages specifically designed for the job. The important thing is to use a method that works for you. You need to be realistic about the amount of time you have to dedicate to what is after all (dare I say it?) simply a hobby. You certainly shouldn't let yourself become a slave to your system, to the extent that keeping your notes properly organised is taking all the fun out of it.

Whether you're using a computer or a paper-based system, you'll soon discover that creating a family tree or a pedigree is an excellent way of bringing all your facts together and illustrating the extent of your knowledge about a particular branch of the family. The tree doesn't have to be an ornate, highly decorative work of art – what's important is that it should be clear and easy to understand. A good family tree should also help you to plan future areas of research by showing gaps in your knowledge.

One good habit that you should get into right from the outset is to make a note of what sources you use in your research. Even if your search was unsuccessful, knowing that the James Smith you found in the 1861 census returns for Little Sodbury is not your man, will stop you from wasting your time repeating the search six months later. It's also good practice to make a note of your sources, so that when you're telling a fellow researcher about a crucial detail relating to your ancestors, or asking for advice from a member of staff in a record office, you can explain how you came to know your 'facts'.

'The Last Will and Testament' of Charles Darwin (died 1882). It was accompanied by a grant of probate, naming executors.

Chapter 6

The will of the people: Probate records

Wills since 1858
Wills before 1858
Interpreting wills
Administrations and inventories
Death duty records
Wills and probate: Some useful terms

Whether your ancestors owned large swathes of land in the north of England or came from a more humble background in the West Country, the chances are that somewhere along the line some of them will have left behind wills, outlining what they wanted to happen to their possessions after their death.

Wills are a truly remarkable source for family historians: not only do they contain invaluable information about family relationships, but the fact that they were written by our ancestors themselves gives them the sort of authority and authenticity that documents created by the government or the Church so often lack.

A couple of crucial points to consider before you start a search for a will. First of all you should be aware that, prior to the passing of the Married Women's Property Act in 1881, you will not, as a rule, find wills for married women, only for widows and spinsters. It's also important to remember that until fairly recent times the vast majority of the population, men or women, simply didn't leave a will. That's not to say that you shouldn't look for one, just that you shouldn't be too surprised if you don't find one.

It's time now to familiarise yourself with another important date on the family history calendar. On 12 January 1858, a new civic system of proving wills (i.e. the process by which a will was accepted as a legally valid document) was introduced. Since medieval times, the responsibility for proving wills had been in the hands of the Church of England, and administered through a vast network of ecclesiastical courts; now the state took over, and district probate registries were set up around the country to handle the process.

So, whenever you're planning a search for an ancestor's will, the first question to ask yourself is whether the person died before or after 1858, and your search will be very different depending on the answer.

Wills since 1858

Searching for a will that was proved on or after 12 January 1858 is a relatively straightforward process. Annual indexes (known as calendars) to all wills proved in England and Wales have been produced right from the start of the civil probate system.

A set of the calendars covering the years 1858 to 1966 is now fully searchable on the Ancestry website but the only complete set of calendars is held by the Principal Registry of the Family Division in their reading rooms at First Avenue House in London.

Some of the district registries also have copies, although many have given their sets to their local county record office. A small number of sets of microfiche covering the years 1858 to 1943 have also been produced. The Society of Genealogists has a set of microfilm copies of the calendars from 1858 to 1930.

The entries in the calendars provide the family historian with some very useful information. A typical entry will tell you:

· the date of probate;
· the deceased's full name;
· their occupation;
· when they died;
· where they died;
· where they lived;
· where the will was proved;

- the names, residences, occupations and relationships of two or more executors;
- the value of the deceased's estate.

Remember, all of this is just from the entry in the calendar. In fact, there isn't a great deal of information on a death certificate that you don't get here, and for this reason many people see little point in spending money on a certificate if they've found a corresponding entry in the will indexes.

However, the deceased's age and the cause of death are crucial details which are not found in the calendars so, if you can, it's really best to get both. In 1892 the format of the calendars changed, and from this date there is significantly less detail in each entry.

Wills before 1858

Before 1858, the situation is much more complicated. There were more than a hundred church courts where wills could be proved; there is no centralised index and the surviving records of the courts are now spread around the country in local and county record offices.

The system was based on the hierarchy of the ancient English ecclesiastical jurisdictions with the provinces of Canterbury and York at the top of the tree, a number of dioceses underneath (each made up of various archdeaconries and deaneries) and with the smaller 'peculiar' courts at the bottom. In practical terms this means that wherever your ancestors lived, their wills could have been proved in one of three or four different courts, and you will have to search the records of each of these in order to establish whether they left a will or not.

The surviving records are likely to include:

- the original wills submitted to the court;
- a series of registered copies entered into ledgers by the court's clerks;
- a set of contemporary manuscript indexes.

Over the years, a number of record offices and local and family history societies have compiled and published various will indexes, and some record offices have produced card indexes to their own holdings. But by far the most significant change in more recent years has been the advent of online probate indexes, in some cases allowing access to digital images of the wills themselves.

The most important of these online resources (and by far the largest) is The National Archives' website at http://www.nationalarchives.gov.uk/records/wills.htm. The website provides full access to the entire collection of wills proved in the Prerogative Court of Canterbury – known more conveniently to family historians as the PCC. This was the senior court of probate for England and Wales, covering the whole of the province of Canterbury – basically the southern two-thirds of England and almost all of Wales. The PCC also had responsibility for the wills of English and Welsh citizens who died overseas or in other parts of the UK.

The collection of over one million wills, dating from 1383 to 1858, includes some of the most famous names in English history: William Shakespeare, Jane Austen, Sir Isaac Newton, Lord Nelson and William Wordsworth, to name but a few. And while it's certainly true that the majority of the wills proved in the PCC relate to people from the upper echelons of society – the nobility and gentry, military officers, merchants, lawyers, clergyman and large landowners – the records also include the wills of many small farmers, artisans, tradesmen, soldiers, sailors and even some agricultural labourers. Perhaps surprisingly, more than a quarter of the wills proved in the PCC are those of women.

The Prerogative Court of York (the PCY) fulfilled a similar role for England's northern counties. The records of the PCY can be seen at the Borthwick Institute in York.

As you move down the hierarchy of ecclesiastical probate courts you'll find increasingly large numbers of wills of 'ordinary' people and, particularly back in the 17th century – in the period before the Industrial Revolution – there's a good chance that you might come across a will or two in the family. If you do, you're in for yet another family history treat.

Interpreting wills

There is simply no limit to the amount of useful detail you could find in a will. At the very least you are likely to get the testator's occupation and place of residence, as well as the names of his wife and children, but you may also discover previously unknown nephews and nieces, uncles, aunts and cousins, and it's not uncommon for more distant relatives to be mentioned. You may also come across references to earlier generations if, for example, the testator refers to an item which was bequeathed to him by a parent or even a grandparent.

As well as providing you with all of this essential information, wills can give you a fascinating insight into your ancestors' lives, often listing personal possessions or tools connected with their trade. Just occasionally, you might come across evidence of a family quarrel where, for example, the eldest son was 'cut off with a shilling' or one of the children was left out of the will altogether, but you need to be careful about how you interpret the size of the bequests. The fact that one child was left significantly less than the others may be because they had already received a sum of money in their father's lifetime.

There are a number of problems that may confront you when you first come to read a will: there's the lack of regular punctuation, the use of archaic terms and the occasional Latin word here or there, but it's probably the unfamiliar handwriting that will cause you the greatest difficulty. The best advice is to get a photocopy of the will and take it home to read at your leisure. Don't try to work out every word first time – if you get stuck on a particular word, carry on and come back to it later. The more you read old wills, the better you will get at recognising the strange characters and styles that were used by the clerks – it really is a matter of experience.

Most wills before 1858 followed a fairly standard format. They usually started with the words 'In the name of God Amen', reflecting both the ecclesiastical background to the process of proving wills and the highly religious nature of the society in which our ancestors lived their lives. Next came the testator's name, occupation and residence, followed by the date of the will and a statement that the testator was either 'in good and perfect health, mind and memory' or possibly 'sick in body but whole in mind' – the important point here was that he was fully rational and compos mentis at the time that the will was written. The testator often left detailed instructions regarding his burial and then, with all these preliminaries out of the way, got on to the real business of the will – making sure that his nearest and dearest got their just deserts.

Working out exactly what the testator was trying to say can be a frustrating process – it's easy to lose track of where you are in a particular sentence as it rambles on into yet another sub clause. It's clear that 18th-century solicitors weren't familiar with the idea of writing in plain English! As we move into the 1800s, wills start to get longer and longer, with increasingly complicated bequests and more and more detailed instructions on how the deceased's estate should be disposed of.

It's a good idea to read through the will, make notes of the various bequests, the places and the personal names that are mentioned in it, and create your own summary. As well as being a useful exercise in itself, this will prove valuable as a quick reference point when planning future research or assessing what you know about the family.

DID YOU KNOW?
The year 1752 saw two major changes to the calendar. Until then, the year had always started on 25 March; now, as part of the adoption of the Gregorian calendar, New Year's Day would be 1 January. Additionally, and more controversially, 11 days were lost in September in order to bring England into line with the rest of Western Europe.

Administrations and inventories

Before we leave the world of probate, there are a couple of other documents to look at that are closely associated with wills. If a person died without leaving a will, letters of administration could be granted to their next of kin or another person who had a claim to the deceased's estate. Letters of administration (commonly known as admons) were granted by the same courts that were responsible for proving wills, with the same change in 1858 from an ecclesiastical to a civil system. In fact, the post-1858 national indexes to admons are combined with the probate calendars, which makes searching for these documents quite straightforward.

Unfortunately for our purposes, the amount of information that you get on letters of administration is quite limited: usually just the name, date of death, residence and occupation of the deceased, as well as the name of the administrator together with their occupation, place of residence and relationship to the deceased. Occasionally there may be some other detail which could provide you with vital information about the family, and it's always worth checking for an admon if your search for a will was unsuccessful. However, you certainly shouldn't assume that because there isn't a will there must be an admon – this is far from being the case.

It was not uncommon before the late 1700s for an inventory to be taken, listing the deceased's personal possessions, often on a room-by-room basis, together with the value of each item and a total value of the estate. And if you're fortunate enough to come across an inventory for a member of your family you should get a fascinating insight into their daily life. Inventories don't survive in huge numbers but, again, it's always worth checking to see if there's one to accompany an ancestor's will.

Death duty records

Both admons and inventories are usually kept together with the collections of wills among the records of the old ecclesiastical courts, but there's another source, closely related to wills, for which we have to thank the Inland Revenue.

A vast series of registers was kept between the years 1796 and 1903 recording the payments of a series of taxes known collectively as death duty. Copies of all wills proved in England and Wales were sent by the various probate courts to the Inland Revenue, where clerks began their work by abstracting the details of the various bequests and beneficiaries and copying the information into their registers.

The death duty registers have a particular value for family historians for a number of reasons. First of all, they identify the name of the court where the will was proved, which in the absence of a pre-1858 national probate index can save you a great deal of searching. Secondly, the registers were living, working documents: the Inland Revenue went to great pains to ensure that they collected every penny due to them, and information about the payments of the duty was recorded meticulously and in great detail.

Therefore, if they learnt that a beneficiary had died, the date of death would be noted; if an executor moved house, the new address was entered; if a daughter married, her married name was recorded.

Sometimes a will might simply indicate that the testator had a number of children, while the equivalent entry in the death duty registers might actually name them. You could even learn about children who were born after the testator wrote his will.

There are, admittedly, a few difficulties that you might encounter with using the registers. For a start, although the indexes are available online (on FindMyPast) you'll need to be able to get to The National Archives in Kew to view the registers themselves.

Secondly, when you do get to see the registers, you'll find that they can be quite difficult to interpret, to say the least. Their very nature, as working documents, can lead to problems. The notes made by the Inland Revenue's clerks, recording the receipt of new information concerning the case, are often written in a heavily abbreviated style which can sometimes obscure their meaning. The clerks clearly knew what they meant at the time but it's not always obvious to us today, and after several years of annotations an entry in the registers can become quite confusing. The entries were only 'closed' once the Inland Revenue were satisfied either that they had collected all the tax due, or that the estate was for one reason or another exempt from payment of duty. And since examples have been found of notes being entered in the registers more than 70 years after an entry was created, you can imagine just how congested the pages can become.

All of these records can be extremely useful in your research, both for the vast amount of information they can provide you with and for the number of other records that they can lead you to. The most obvious are records of deaths and burials, but they can also suggest links to census returns, births and baptisms, marriages and even more 'advanced' sources concerning land ownership and legal disputes. Wills are a vital resource for family historians, and although accessing and interpreting the records may present you with some difficulties, you should make every possible effort to track them down and take the time to learn what they're telling us about the lives of our ancestors.

Wills and probate: Some useful terms

Administrator	A person who is appointed to administer the estate of an *intestate* or to administer in default of an executor named in a will. A woman appointed in this way is known as an *administratrix*.
Annuity	An income or allowance received annually.
Appurtenances	Something that belongs to something else. For example, the land in which a house is situated.
Assign or assignee	A person who is appointed to act in place of another, often found in the phrase 'heirs and assigns'.
Beneficiary	A person who is left something in a will.
Codicil	A supplement to a will.
Executor	A person appointed by the testator to ensure that his wishes are carried out. A female appointed in this way is known as an *executrix*.
Heir	The person who is legally entitled to succeed to another's property.
Hereditaments	Property that can be inherited.
Imprimis	First (Latin)
Intestate	A person who dies without leaving a will.
Item	Further (Latin)
Messuage	A house or dwelling-place together with its *appurtenances*.
Personal estate	A person's moveable property, not including land and buildings etc.
Probate	Proving a will. The act of making it a legally binding document.
Real estate	The land and buildings etc. (i.e. not moveable property) owned by a person.
Testator	A man who makes a will. A woman is known as a *testatrix*.

Check it out

The idea of indexing records which might be of interest to family historians is hardly a new one. As we have already seen, the documents we use in our research were not designed with us in mind, nor are they necessarily arranged in a way that makes it easy for us to find the information we're looking for. In order to address this problem there has been a huge effort over the years on the part of record offices and archives, commercial organisations, record societies, family and local history groups and hundreds of dedicated individuals to make the records we use more accessible.

In recent years the progress in this area has been remarkable. Indeed the existence of global search engines such as Google has blurred the boundaries: nowadays just about any material which is available online is automatically 'indexed' by Google. And this is true whether the source is a traditional family history one or not.

The work of indexing the records that we use today began in earnest during the 19th century, when enthusiastic antiquarians started to recognise the importance of Britain's vast wealth of historical records and set about the task of preserving them for posterity. Documents like parish registers, poll books, tax returns and medieval legal records were among the most popular records for the antiquarians to tackle.

In the 1970s and 1980s the focus moved to indexing census returns and wills, and family history societies were particularly active in producing census indexes for their own areas of interest. Using a vast army of volunteers, almost 80 per cent of the returns for 1851 were indexed, along with large sections of the other years. In the mid 1980s a project to index the 1881 census returns for the whole of England, Wales and Scotland began, involving the combined efforts of the Church of Jesus Christ of Latter-day Saints (the Mormons), the Federation of Family History Societies and the Public Record Office, and despite taking over 10 years to complete, it showed the family history world that such a mammoth task was possible and helped to establish certain standards and principles for future indexing projects.

The Mormons are also behind what is surely the single most significant index for family historians. FamilySearch brings together several hundred million records of births, baptisms, marriages and burials, mainly extracted from parish registers. Every serious family historian will at some time in the course of their research have cause to consult FamilySearch – it is quite simply indispensable and it's free!

To anyone who was involved in family history before the digital revolution, the achievement of the major commercial family history websites in creating comprehensive indexes to such vast collections of records is simply astonishing. Particularly when compared to the piecemeal efforts of individuals and volunteer groups. But perhaps the biggest breakthrough has been the ability to link search results to digital images of the original records.

An index on its own is simply a means of helping the user to identify potentially useful documents, not a replacement for viewing the records themselves. You need to view the document itself (the original, a microfilm copy or in digital form) to be sure that what the index is telling you is actually true. You should never rely on what you find in an index alone – instead, you should use the information as a way into the documents. The index may contain errors – after all, the person who transcribed the details from the original may not have been entirely familiar with the handwriting or with the names of the people or places. But, more importantly, the original may contain additional information – information which may give you vital clues about your ancestors.

Page from the parish register of St Chad's, Shrewsbury, showing the baptism of Charles Darwin, 1809.

Chapter 7

Parcels of the past: Records before 1837

Assuming that you've had a successful passage through the records we've looked at in the previous chapters, you should now have reached the point where you're searching for an ancestor who was born prior to the start of civil registration in 1837. And provided that you've done your research thoroughly and you've used the records to their full potential, you should by now have enough information on your ancestor to fully arm yourself for the big adventure that's about to begin.

A brief history of parish registers

In 1538, King Henry VIII's chief minister Thomas Cromwell ordered that registers should be kept recording all the baptisms, marriages and burials that took place in each parish. There were some early teething problems – many parsons, vicars and curates were unsure about exactly what information was to be recorded, and although the entries were supposed to be made in a register book, many ended up on loose sheets of paper. In 1598 a further order was approved by Queen Elizabeth in an attempt to tighten up the system. Parchment registers were to be purchased by every parish and duplicate copies of the entries were to be sent to the relevant bishop's court. At the same time the details from the earlier registers were supposed to be copied into these new bound registers. However, many clerks ignored the first 20 years and started in 1558 (the first year of Queen Elizabeth's reign) and fewer than 1,000 registers are known to start as early as 1538. Only a handful of Welsh parish registers commence in the 16th century.

The duplicate copies (known as bishops' transcripts) have survived in large numbers to the present day and are usually held by diocesan record offices – which in most cases are also the county record offices. As well as being an important alternative source for family historians, these transcripts acted as a useful measure against fraud – after all, there's very little point in altering an entry in the local parish register if the bishop has his own copy securely stored away.

Most of the earliest surviving registers are composite registers, covering baptisms, marriages and burials in a single volume, and the entries in them are somewhat lacking in detail. Each entry consists of the date of the event followed by the most basic information: the baptisms rarely recorded more than the name of the child and the father's name, the marriages would usually give the names of both parties but are unlikely to tell you anything else about them, while the burial entries often consisted of nothing more than the name of the deceased.

Latin in parish registers

Many early parish registers were written in Latin, but this shouldn't present too big a problem as most of the entries are in a fairly standard format.

Important Latin words in family history records

son	*filius*	married	*in matrimonium ducere*
daughter	*filia*	buried	*sepultus*
wife	*uxor*	age in years	*aetatis*
father	*pater*	widow	*vidue*
mother	*mater*	deceased	*defuncti*
baptised	*baptisatus*		

Remember that Latin words have different endings depending on the context and on whether the subject is male or female – for example, the Latin for buried is *sepultus* but if the person being buried was female, the word used would be *sepulta*. Even personal names can have different endings – the name Robert in Latin is *Robertus* but 'Robert, son of Robert' would be *Robertus filius Roberti*. There are many useful books and websites which cover this subject in much greater depth.

Later parish registers

Gradually, the amount of detail in the registers increased: it became normal to show the mother's name on baptisms, marriages would show the bride or groom's parish if they were marrying away from home and burial entries recording the age of the deceased started to become more common.

During the 17th and early 18th centuries, increasingly large numbers of people began to marry outside the established Church of England. By the late 1740s the government had become seriously concerned about the problem of so-called clandestine or irregular marriages, which, although perfectly legal, were usually conducted by disreputable clergymen and were open to all sorts of abuse and fraud. Most took place in one of a number of notorious venues in London such as the precincts of the Fleet Prison, the Mayfair Chapel and Holy Trinity Minories, and since there was little or no control over them, bigamous marriages were quite common.

In order to deal with this growing problem, Hardwicke's Marriage Act was passed by Parliament. By the terms of this Act, which came into force in 1754, only marriages conducted according to the 'rites and ceremonies' of the Church of England would be recognised in law. All marriages now had to be performed in one of two ways – either after banns or by licence. And they had to be recorded in a dedicated marriage register with individually numbered entries – a means of ensuring that the details were properly recorded and an effective safeguard against fraud. So from 1754 until the start of civil registration in 1837, unless your ancestors were Jewish or Quakers (both were specifically exempted from the terms of Hardwicke's Act), you should expect to find their marriages recorded in the Church of England's parish registers.

The registers show the names of the bride and groom as well as their parish of residence and their marital status. If either of them was a minor (i.e. aged under 21) this will be recorded, and the register will always show whether the marriage was by licence or banns. You will also find the signatures (or marks) of both parties, together with the signatures of two or more witnesses – and remember that the signatures you see here were actually written by your ancestors, perhaps as long as 250 years ago.

In 1813, pre-printed registers were introduced for baptisms and burials, and from this date the entries in most parish registers are of a standard format. The baptismal registers recorded the following details:

· when baptised
· child's Christian name
· parents' names:
  – Christian
  – surname
· abode
· quality, trade or profession
· by whom the ceremony was performed

Much of this information is the same as you would expect to find on the post-1837 civil registration birth certificates – the only two details which are lacking here are the date of birth and the mother's maiden name.

In fact, the date of birth is quite often entered in the registers, particularly in cases of multiple baptisms where two or more children from the same family were baptised at the same time. And although most children were baptised when they were only a month or two old, it's important to bear in mind that the baptism could take place several months or even years later.

The pre-printed burial registers from 1813 onwards provided the following information:

· name
· abode
· when buried
· age
· by whom the ceremony was performed

As you can see, the amount of information here is fairly limited. There's no space for the deceased's occupation (which was sometimes given in burial registers before 1813) and, more importantly, there's nothing whatsoever about the deceased's relationship to anyone else. But in most cases there should be enough to enable you to identify your ancestors.

The middle of the 19th century saw the advent of municipal cemeteries, and in most urban areas you shouldn't expect to find too many church burials after about 1855. Some cemetery registers have been deposited with county record offices but most are still in the care of the cemeteries themselves, while many are held by the relevant local authorities. The pre-printed registers which were introduced in 1813 are still in use today, and although after 1837 they are not generally considered a major source for family historians, they certainly shouldn't be ignored.

Parish registers do have certain advantages over the equivalent civil registration records. For a start, the registers are held locally (normally in the appropriate county record office) where access to them is both straightforward and free. Secondly, parish registers now appear to be at the top of the list of family history sources for the major commercial websites to index and digitise. Ancestry has already made large collections of registers from London, Liverpool, West Yorkshire and Dorset available on their website and it's certain that more will follow.

Dade registers

If you're very lucky, you may find that your ancestors came from a parish where a special type of register, known as a Dade register, was in use. Named after the Reverend William Dade, the man who was primarily responsible for their introduction, the registers are a gold mine for family historians. Dade baptism registers normally record not only the child's name and parents' names, but also their position in the family (i.e. first son, second daughter and so on) along with details of both sets of grandparents and sometimes additional information about the parents, such as their places of birth. Dade burial registers normally give the deceased's parents' names, and you may even find the cause of death given. Unfortunately, these registers are primarily from parishes in Yorkshire but there are also a few from

Lancashire, Nottinghamshire and Cheshire, and similar registers are occasionally found in parts of Wiltshire, Somerset and Berkshire.

Before you start

There are a few questions that you'll need to ask yourself before you start searching for your ancestors in parish registers. For example, if you're looking for a baptism, do you have all the information you need to carry out an effective search? Do you know:

· approximately when they were born?
· where they were born?
· their father's name?

If the person you're looking for was born in the first few decades of the 19th century then you'll probably have all this from the research you've done previously – you should have their age and place of birth from the censuses and their father's name from their marriage certificate. But once you start working further back in time you'll soon find that identifying the correct entry becomes increasingly difficult.

The biggest problem you'll come up against is knowing where to search for your ancestors, because they had an annoying habit of moving around from village to village! Once you get back into the 18th century, you won't have census returns to help track their movements.

But if not, all is not lost: for over 100 years the Church of Jesus Christ of Latter-day Saints (the Mormons) have been extracting information from parish registers, and the result of their labour is now available as part of the world's biggest family history database – FamilySearch.

FamilySearch

FamilySearch is a vast database containing several hundred million records – mainly births, baptisms, marriages and burials extracted from parish registers. In fact, FamilySearch is a worldwide database consisting of over 1,000 separate record collections, many of which include links to digital images of the original records. At the time of writing, the main English collections cover nearly 70 million births and baptisms, 16 million marriages and 15 million deaths and burials.

In addition to this 'national' database, FamilySearch also includes significant collections covering specific counties such as Cheshire, Durham, Norfolk and Warwickshire.

FamilySearch is without doubt the most indispensable of resources for family historians all around the world, but you should always bear in mind that it is by no means a comprehensive record. Its coverage is patchy, to say the least: some parts of the country are well served, while others have relatively few entries. You should never assume that the absence of an entry for your ancestor means that he or she wasn't baptised. If the parish where they were born isn't covered by FamilySearch then you wouldn't expect to find a record of their baptism there. And if you find an entry which looks quite promising but doesn't quite fit, try to resist the temptation to accept the entry as yours, and consider the possibility that your ancestor might simply have been baptised in a neighbouring parish which isn't covered by the database.

Having said all this, FamilySearch should always be your first port of call once you arrive in the pre-civil registration era. When you find an entry which appears to relate to your ancestor, the first thing you need to do is to ask yourself whether you can prove 'beyond reasonable doubt' that the entry you've found is the right one. If the name you're looking for is relatively uncommon, or if you're working with a very distinctive middle name, your search will be that much easier. Don't forget to consider all the issues regarding names that we looked at in the chapter on births (Chapter 2, see pages 17–30), and it's particularly important to remember that the further back you go, the more you need to be on the lookout for alternative spellings of names – first names as well as surnames.

FamilySearch is particularly useful on this last point, as it groups similar names together. So whether your ancestor is recorded as Robert or Robt., a search should find him. It also includes Latin forms of names, so Robertus would show up too. Surnames work in the same way: a search for the name Hibbert would bring up alternative spellings such as Hibbard, Hibbart and Hebbard, as well as less obvious variants like Ibbett, Ibbots and Hibarte. You do have the option to search for exact spellings of names but in most cases this is not advisable.

Other parish register indexes

FamilySearch isn't the only index that you can use to help you with your parish register searches. The major commercial websites (particularly Ancestry and FindMyPast) each have their own parish register databases and are certain to add to their collections over the next few years.

There are also two dedicated marriage indexes which you will almost certainly find helpful in your research. Pallot's Marriage Index was started by a firm of record agents in 1813 and contains 1.5 million marriages. It's particularly strong for London and Middlesex, but it also has many thousands of entries from other parts of the country. The index covers the years 1780 to 1837 and is practically complete in this period for the city of London. Pallot's Index is available on the Ancestry website.

Family historians have many reasons to be grateful to the late Percival Boyd. Boyd began his greatest project in 1925 and the result is an index to more than six million marriage entries taken from parish registers the length and breadth of the country. It covers the years 1538 to 1837 and has excellent coverage for certain counties, such as Cambridgeshire, Essex and Suffolk, although in some cases there are few entries after 1753. Boyd's Marriage Index is available on FindMyPast. There are also hundreds of smaller marriage indexes compiled by family history societies, local record offices and enterprising individuals.

The National Burial Index (NBI), now in its third edition, contains over 18 million burial records dating from the earliest years of parish registers right up to the 21st century. The vast majority of the records, however, relate to burials from the early to mid 1800s. The database consists of transcribed entries from parish, nonconformist and cemetery registers and, as with all indexes which do not provide direct links to digital images of their source material, you should always check the original entry. Remember, an index is not a primary source. Much of the NBI is online at FindMypast.co.uk.

Very few parish registers (other than the ones that are still in use) are held in parish churches. The vast majority have been deposited in the relevant county record office, although some are held in local studies libraries. There are a number of excellent resources which will tell you where the original registers are held, and the best is *The Phillimore Atlas & Index of Parish Registers*. Now in its third edition, this essential tome is known to many as the bible of family historians. The atlas is divided into two sections; the first includes a series of maps (one for each English county, three covering Wales) showing the location of each ancient parish together with the starting dates of the earliest surviving parish registers. For each county there is also a separate topographical map dating from 1834 showing the main roads and other features, which should help you to place your ancestor's village or town in its local context.

The second section consists of a series of county lists that record a remarkable amount of information for each parish, including the earliest and latest dates of its deposited registers; the coverage in FamilySearch and various other marriage indexes; and the name of the relevant civil registration district. These lists also act as an index to the maps and, most important of all, they indicate where the original parish registers are now held. The latest edition of *The Phillimore Atlas & Index of Parish Registers* also includes a similar series of parish maps and county lists for Scotland.

Another excellent source is the multi-volume *National Index of Parish Registers,* which lists, county by county, all the known surviving parish registers together with their covering dates, information about indexes, copies and transcripts and the whereabouts of the originals.

Many county record offices have put lists of their parish register holdings online, and their websites may be more up to date than the printed sources, listing newly deposited registers and other recent acquisitions. Many local studies centres and larger libraries also hold copies of the parish registers for their own areas, and the Society of Genealogists has a huge collection of microfilms and transcripts of literally thousands of parish registers. The Society's online catalogue lists their parish register holdings: http://62.32.98.6/S10312UKStaff/OPAC/.

As well as indexing millions of records from parish registers, the Church of Jesus Christ of Latter-day Saints has also undertaken a huge microfilming programme, and you can access copies of thousands of English and Welsh parish registers through their family history centres. The London Family History Centre (currently located at The National Archives, Kew) has a particularly good collection of parish register material which can be searched on their catalogue at www.londonfhc. org/content/catalogue. Regional family history centres naturally have much smaller collections but any Latter-day Saints' microfilm can be ordered to be viewed at any Latter-day Saints' FamilySearch history centre. You'll have to pay a small fee and wait a week or two for the microfilm to arrive, but if your ancestors lived hundreds of miles away and you can't easily get to the relevant county record office, this may be a cheaper and more convenient option for you.

Searching in parish registers

If the registers you need to search haven't been indexed then you'll have to grit your teeth and prepare for what could be a long and challenging search. The post-1812 registers are fairly easy to search (although in the bigger urban parishes, finding as many as 50 baptisms being performed each week is not at all uncommon, so you may still be in for a lengthy search) but the earlier registers can be quite troublesome. The general standard of handwriting leaves a lot to be desired, and in many cases you'll find baptisms and burials and sometimes even marriages mixed in together on the same page.

The best approach is not to rush your search – it's so easy to miss a vital entry if you're not concentrating properly or if you're scanning a page too quickly. It's a good idea, particularly if you're searching in a rural area, to make a note of any entries you happen upon with the surname that you're looking for. If it's a common name you may find too many entries, most of which have no connection whatsoever to your family, but if you're dealing with a fairly uncommon name, any instance of it in your ancestor's parish is worth noting, as it may turn out to be a relative. You should certainly note down any siblings of your direct ancestors that you come across – it all helps to build up the picture of your ancestors' lives in the parish and, of course, the baptism of the first child will help you in your search for the parents' marriage.

An important point to bear in mind when searching for a marriage (if you haven't been able to find it in one of the various indexes we've looked at) is that the couple normally married in the bride's parish. Until fairly recent times, only a small minority of people moved more than about twenty miles from their place of birth during the course of their lives. They may have moved frequently from one village to another seeking work, but they tended to stay within their own 'country', an area centred on a market town which served as both a trading post and a meeting place. The regular markets, with their gatherings of farmers, tradesmen and labourers, provided a great opportunity for people from different villages to meet and get to know each other. This would have been the way that many of our ancestors met their future husbands and wives, and it helps to explain why men so often ended up marrying women from relatively distant parishes. It was also fairly common for women to return to their home parish for their first confinement, so you may find that the oldest child was baptised in a different parish from the rest.

By far the biggest problem with searching in parish registers is that there is absolutely nothing in them which explicitly links one record to another. A baptism will show the names of the child's parents but not its mother's maiden name, so identifying a corresponding marriage may be a difficult task. And while it may be obvious that the marriage of John Wilkinson and Mary Brown that you found in 1785 ties in with the baptisms of those children of John and Mary Wilkinson in the same parish starting in 1786, if the children had all been born in different parishes you might have had some difficulty tracking them down. And if you were coming at the problem from the opposite direction, and had found the baptisms of these children, proving that they all belonged to the same family would be far from straightforward.

There are a number of techniques you can use to help overcome these problems. The most useful is a method known as family reconstitution, which involves extracting all the references to a particular surname from the registers of a specific parish or a number of neighbouring parishes over a number of years and using the information to build up likely family groups. This research can then be backed up with information from other sources such as wills, manorial documents and legal records. It's not a foolproof process and it can be very time consuming, but it's often the only approach that will produce results.

In the 300 years before the start of civil registration, parish registers represent the single most important source for family historians. There were over 12,000 ancient parishes in England and Wales, and the registers kept by those parishes are a vast and unique collection, recording the lives of many millions of English and Welsh men and women over nearly 500 years of our history. The fact that they have survived the ravages of time is testament to the relative stability that the country has known over this period. With the notable exception of the English Civil War in the middle of the 17th century, there have been no major interruptions to the process of recording the vital events in our ancestors' lives.

When the system of registers was first set up in 1538 the intention was to record every baptism, marriage and burial taking place within each parish; however, the rise of English Protestant nonconformity meant that the registers ceased to be a complete record of these events as more and more people moved to new places of worship, and away from the established Church of England.

DID YOU KNOW?
The phrase 'of full age' which is frequently found on marriage certificates in the early years of civil registration means that the person in question was aged 21 years or more.

Family, friends and neighbours

There are two main ways of drawing up a family tree: you can either start from yourself and work upwards, or start with your oldest known ancestor and work down through the generations. Neither method is intrinsically 'better' than the other, but there's a real danger that if you only use the bottom-up (pedigree) method to record the results of your research, you're not really looking at the whole picture. Pedigrees only show your direct ancestors – your parents, grandparents, great-grandparents and so on. Brothers and sisters, nephews and nieces, aunts, uncles and cousins are nowhere to be seen, and yet if you're not fully investigating them and their lives, it's not really a family history at all.

Finding out about these relatives, getting to know more about your ancestors' extended families, is a great way to increase your knowledge of the family as a whole and to help you get a better understanding of what your ancestors' lives were really like. And if you're only looking at your direct ancestors, you may miss some vital clues.

You should really aim to track down all of your ancestors' siblings in each of the census returns. Information about their ages, places of birth and occupations can point you in unexpected directions or suggest new areas of interesting research. An uncle's will might mention your direct ancestor – as a beneficiary or even an executor – and your great-great-grandfather might have been a witness at the wedding of one of his brothers or sisters. So while you may concentrate the main efforts of your research on your direct lines, you should never ignore the other family members and the additional information that the records of their lives can add to the story of your family.

And you shouldn't ignore your ancestors' neighbours, either. The people that your family rubbed shoulders with, day in, day out, almost certainly had a significant impact on their lives. When you find your ancestors in the census returns, you should make a point of looking at the other families living nearby. The occupations will give you an idea of the sort of area they lived in – and it's possible that the neighbours were also relatives, not just in rural areas. Even in large towns and cities it wasn't at all uncommon to find siblings, cousins or in-laws living next door. Family history is not about individuals: it's about families and the communities that they lived in. And when you start to extend your research beyond the immediate family your efforts will be richly rewarded.

Page from the Presbyterian Chapel register, Shrewsbury, showing the baptism of Catherin Emily Darwin (Charles Darwin's sister), 1810.

Chapter 8

Other directions:
More record sources

Nonconformist registers
Other associated registers
Dr Williams's Library
The Wesleyan Methodist Metropolitan Registry
The Fleet Marriage Registers
Roman Catholic records
Jewish records

The history of English nonconformity can be traced back as far as the 14th century. But it wasn't until the second half of the 17th century that groups of likeminded 'dissenters' started to become organised and to develop their own identities.

The term 'nonconformist' is generally used to describe any Protestant who does not conform to the doctrines and usages of the established Church of England. By the start of the 19th century, nonconformists made up around a quarter of the population of England and Wales. This figure has a significant impact on our family history research, since it would suggest that the baptisms of as many as a quarter of our ancestors won't be recorded in the Church of England's parish registers.

Over the years a number of distinct groups emerged: Quakers, Baptists, Independents (also known as Congregationalists), Presbyterians, Methodists, Unitarians and many more. Each had their own individual beliefs (mostly to do with how the church should be run rather than any major doctrinal differences) but the boundaries between the various denominations were often quite blurred; groups merged with each other or split off to form new sects. Some of the groups had hundreds of places of worship around the country, with huge numbers of people attending their weekly services, while other smaller denominations such as the Swedenborgians, the Inghamites and the Moravians consisted of just a few scattered congregations.

Swelling the ranks of these dissenting groups were large numbers of Protestant immigrants who settled in England from the 16th century onwards. The most significant of these were the Huguenots: French Calvinists who fled to England to escape persecution in their own country. The Huguenots settled mainly in the East End of London, but there were also significant communities in several other towns and cities in the south and east of England, most notably Norwich, Plymouth and Canterbury. Calvinist exiles from the Netherlands also founded their own congregations in the south of England in the late 16th century.

Nonconformist registers

In 1837, as part of the establishment of the civil registration system, a Commission was set up and the surviving registers of all these nonconformist congregations were called in by the newly formed General Register Office. Not all of the congregations complied with the request to surrender their registers (and it wasn't compulsory) but most did; and eventually, following a further call in 1858, over 6,000 registers were collected. The entire collection (properly known as the 'Non-parochial' registers since some of the registers originally belonged to Anglican organisations) was later transferred to the Public Record Office (now The National Archives).

Very few of these registers date from before the Civil War period and it's unlikely that any of the English nonconformist congregations kept registers before then. The earliest registers in The National Archives' collection are those of the Protestant immigrant communities; the oldest, dating from 1567, is from the Southampton 'Walloon' church. The register of Hindley Presbyterian Church, Lancashire, is the earliest surviving English Protestant nonconformist register, with entries dating from 1642.

The standard of record-keeping differed greatly from one denomination to another. By far the best in terms of detail, accuracy and completeness are those of the Religious Society of Friends or, as they are more commonly known, the Quakers. The National Archives has copies of around 1,500 registers of births, deaths, burials and marriages of Quaker congregations from every corner of England and Wales. This is the largest collection of any single denomination, and when the records were catalogued by the Public Record Office they were placed in a distinct series of their own.

The registers of the Moravian Church represent another good example of meticulous record-keeping, and in addition to the usual records of baptisms, marriages and burials, many of them contain a wealth of information about the history and administration of the congregation. This is a feature of many nonconformist registers: lists of ministers and members of the congregations, plans of churches and burial grounds, financial transactions, trust deeds, even transcripts of wills – all of these and more can be found in these registers. If you find a record of your ancestor in a nonconformist register, don't just note the details of their baptism and move on to the next task on your list – it's always worth having a look at the rest of the register to see if any extra information is included.

As a rule, from 1754 the registers only contain records of baptisms and burials – under the terms of Hardwicke's Marriage Act, nonconformists were forced to marry within the established Church of England. However, Quakers were specifically exempted from this Act and the records of Quaker marriages are among the most extraordinary documents that you'll come across. As well as details of the bride and groom and the names and occupations of their parents, Quaker marriage certificates often include the names of as many as 50 witnesses, many of whom were probably relatives of the couple.

Since relatively few of the congregations had their own burial grounds, many nonconformists were buried in the Anglican parish churchyard, but most chose to have their children baptised in their own churches and chapels. Nonconformist registers are generally more informative than their Anglican counterparts – the baptismal registers often recorded the mother's maiden name – but the amount of information included differs so much from one denomination to another, and even among different congregations of the same denomination, that it's probably best just to say that you'll find out when you get there!

Most of the registers held by The National Archives end in 1837, although the second commission of 1858 resulted in the deposit of another 500 or so registers. And don't forget that the congregations continued to keep records of baptisms, burials and marriages (which could again take place in nonconformist chapels from 1 July 1837) beyond this date. Many of these later registers have been deposited in local or county record offices but some are still in the care of the congregations.

DID YOU KNOW?

Family history research is an important part of the doctrine of the Church of Jesus Christ of Latter-day Saints – the Mormon church. The Mormons have devoted considerable resources to gathering records, producing invaluable tools for the family historian: notably the FamilySearch database. Church members use these resources to make 'covenants' on behalf of their deceased ancestors.

Other associated registers

As well as the records of the many individual nonconformist congregations, there are also several collections of registers of large multi-denominational burial grounds, such as Bunhill Fields, the Victoria Park Cemetery, Gibraltar Row, Golden Lane Cemetery and Southwark New Burial Ground in London, and the wonderfully named Necropolis Burial Ground in Liverpool.

Along with all these nonconformist registers, the General Register Office collected a number of registers that belonged to the Anglican Church but which were outside the normal parochial system. These include the registers of the British Lying-in Hospital in Holborn, the Greenwich and Chelsea Hospitals (for the Royal Navy and Army respectively) and other smaller institutions such as Mercers' Hall in Cheapside, London, and the Chapels Royal at Whitehall and Windsor.

Before we leave the subject of nonconformists and the records that they left behind, there are some other significant collections of records to consider.

Dr Williams's Library

Two Acts of Parliament which were passed in the late 17th century effectively prevented Protestant nonconformists and Roman Catholics from holding official positions in England and Wales. The Test and

Corporation Acts meant that only people who had been baptised according to the rites and ceremonies of the established Church of England could sit on town councils, hold commissions in the Army and Royal Navy, or teach at or even attend universities. In 1727 the General Body of Ministers of the Three Denominations was established to represent the views of the Presbyterians, Baptists and Independents (or Congregationalists) in the campaign for the repeal of the Test and Corporation Acts. The campaign was eventually successful, although it wasn't until 1828 that the Acts were overturned and nonconformists gained full religious freedom. One of the many grievances that nonconformists held was that their baptismal registers had no legal standing and were not recognised by courts of law in matters of inheritance or intestacy.

In 1742, as a small but significant part of their long campaign for religious equality, the Three Denominations started their own birth registry. The idea was to demonstrate that they could record birth details, issue certificates and produce accurate copies of these certificates – all in a highly efficient way and with an exceptional standard of record-keeping. Initially, very few births were registered – only 309 are recorded in the first 26 years of the registry – but by the time the registry was closed in December 1837 it included the details of almost 50,000 births. The registry was officially called the General Register of Protestant Dissenters, but over the years it has come to be known in the family history world as 'Dr Williams's Library' – named after the building in which it was housed from 1742 until 1837. It's an unfortunately misleading name, as not only does it not describe what the registry actually was, but it causes all sorts of problems for the staff of Dr Williams's Library, which is still in existence today. The registers are no longer held by the Library but were deposited with the General Register Office in the late 1830s and are now held by The National Archives.

The registry produced three different sets of documents: the original birth registers, a complete collection of the certificates issued by the registry and a set of contemporary indexes. One of the reasons that the records are so useful for family historians is that retrospective registration was actively encouraged. The registry was opened in 1742 but the earliest birth recorded dates from 1716 and several registrations have been found of people aged 50 or more.

If you're lucky enough to have ancestors whose births were registered in the General Register of Protestant Dissenters you really are in for a treat. In addition to the usual information that you might expect to find with a birth or baptism – the child's name, place and date of birth and the parents' names – you will usually get not just the mother's maiden name but also the names of her parents. All of this information should be fully recorded both on the copy certificates and in the registers, but it's always worth checking both sources as you may find that one contains more information than the other.

The Wesleyan Methodist Metropolitan Registry

In 1818 the Wesleyan Methodists started a very similar registry known as the Wesleyan Methodist Metropolitan Registry. The methods of record-keeping and the types of records created were essentially identical to those used by the Three Denominations in their registry, and although the Methodists' birth registry is somewhat smaller it does contain over 10,000 records, so it still represents a significant collection. The registry was officially closed in December 1837 but the final entry in the records was made on 7 January 1840.

The Fleet Marriage Registers

This is one of the most curious collections of registers held by The National Archives, with a strange and chequered history. The registers were originally kept by the clergymen who performed the marriage ceremonies and were, in effect, their personal property. When Hardwicke's Marriage Act became law in 1754, the various marriage chapels were closed down, and at this stage many of the registers are thought to have been destroyed or simply lost.

However, a few enterprising individuals began to gather together the surviving registers (many of which are in fact no more than rough notebooks) and in 1821 the collection was purchased by the government. They eventually ended up in the Public Record Office and were grouped together with the larger collections of nonconformist registers. But they are in fact Anglican registers, recording the marriages of individuals who were married, perfectly legally, 'according to the rites and ceremonies of the established Church'.

The problem with them is that they were so open to abuse, and by their very nature the registers are of questionable authenticity. There is evidence that details have been altered, names and dates changed and entirely false entries created. But despite their potentially spurious nature, you certainly shouldn't ignore the Fleet Registers: it has been estimated that half of all marriages in London in the 1740s and early 1750s took place in this way, in or around the Fleet Prison in London or at the Mayfair Chapel in Westminster. The surviving registers record around 350,000 marriages. One rather surprising aspect of the Fleet Marriage Registers is that they also include a significant number of baptisms!

Accessing the records

And now for some good news: The National Archives' entire collection of 'non-parochial' registers, including the registers of the Huguenot congregations, the General Register of Protestant Dissenters (commonly known as Dr Williams's Library), the Wesleyan Methodist Metropolitan Register, the Fleet Marriage Registers and the various multi-denominational cemetery registers, has been digitised, indexed and made available online. The BMD Registers website (www. bmdregisters.co.uk) provides access to the registers with links to digital images of the original documents. This database is one of the best examples of the benefits of 21st-century online indexing. The registers were brought together from a variety of unrelated sources and, due to their irregular nature, they were once very difficult to access. Searches in the registers tended to be speculative at best and their contents were therefore effectively inaccessible to most researchers. Nowadays, searching couldn't be easier and the records have become the invaluable resource that they always should have been.

Many of the Protestant registers collected by the first Commission in 1837 are also covered by the FamilySearch database, so if you find a reference to an event which appears to have taken place in a non-Anglican church it probably relates to one of these registers.

Roman Catholic records

The National Archives' collection of nonconformist records also includes a small number of Roman Catholic registers. There was significant resistance among the Catholic clergy to the General Register

Office's registration commission and in the end only 77 congregations surrendered their registers. The bulk of these are from Yorkshire.

A detailed description of the history of Roman Catholicism in England and Wales is well beyond the scope of a book of this nature. But it is important to understand that for long periods between the English Reformation of 1534 and the passing of the Roman Catholic Relief Act in 1829, Catholicism was actively suppressed and its followers were sometimes ruthlessly persecuted. As a result of this persecution, Roman Catholics were understandably reluctant to record and publish records of their activities, which goes some way to explaining the relative scarcity of surviving records – particularly from the early years. Although many anti-Catholic laws remained in place, from 1689 onwards they were rarely enforced and Catholics were largely free to celebrate mass and perform baptisms.

There are several excellent sources which will help those of you with Catholic ancestors to locate the whereabouts of the surviving records. The most important of these is Michael Gandy's six-volume series *Catholic Missions and Registers 1700–1880* (see page 182 for details), which lists all known surviving Roman Catholic registers, together with their covering dates and their current whereabouts.

Jewish records

The history of the Jews in England and Wales is even more problematic. The modern Jewish community in this country can trace its history back to the middle of the 17th century when Sephardic Jews (those from Italy, Spain and Portugal) started to arrive here, soon to be followed by Ashkenazim (from the Netherlands and Eastern Europe). The last few decades of the 19th century saw a huge influx of Jews from Russia and Poland. But since the births, marriages and deaths of our Jewish ancestors are fully covered by the General Register Office's civil registration process and Jewish families are recorded in the census returns in exactly the same way as the rest of the population, the modern records of these later immigrants are no different to those of our Anglican and nonconformist ancestors. Finding out exactly where in Eastern Europe they came from may be a difficult task, and one that is tied up with records of immigration and naturalisation. Roger Kershaw and Mark Pearsall's book *Immigrants and Aliens* (see page 183 for details) is an excellent starting point for research in this area.

As a general rule, the records of the various Jewish communities in England and Wales are held by the relevant congregations. However, many records, including those of the Great Synagogue and the New Synagogue in London, which start as early as 1791, have been microfilmed and can be viewed at Latter-day Saints' family history centres. As has been mentioned before, Jews were exempted from the terms of Hardwicke's Marriage Act and therefore marriages which took place in the Jewish faith between 1754 and 1837 are legally valid. The JewishGen website (www.jewishgen.org) is an excellent resource for Jewish family history. The site includes a searchable database which is rapidly growing into an invaluable tool for those with Jewish ancestry. The Jewish Genealogical Society of Great Britain is very active in promoting the use and understanding of specifically Jewish records in family history research. If you are serious about researching your own Jewish ancestors, you should consider joining them.

Be prepared

These are the words that Scouts learn when they join their first troop, but the phrase is equally appropriate for family historians. If you're about to make your first trip to a record office or archive you really should prepare thoroughly for your visit.

First of all you need to know the basics about the office you're poised to descend upon. What are its opening hours? Do you need to book in advance? Do you need to bring any identification with you? Does the archive actually have the records that you want to see and do you need to order anything in advance? So many visits to record offices end up in disappointment simply because the researcher hasn't done their groundwork properly.

Find out if you can obtain photocopies of the documents you're planning to look at. Can you bring a laptop or a digital camera? If you intend to take notes, you will certainly need to bring a pencil – pens and archives just don't mix! Bags aren't welcome in reading rooms either, but most record offices provide lockers and a refreshment/cloakroom area – it's worth checking whether you need to bring a coin for the lockers.

And let's dispel straight away the image of archives as dark and dusty, oak-panelled, cobwebbed reading rooms, staffed by frightening, dusty, cobwebbed archivists. Most record offices these days are located in well-equipped, modern buildings with excellent facilities including state-of-the-art IT equipment. The staff are well trained, knowledgeable and friendly, and you'll find that many are active family historians themselves.

Don't be frightened of asking questions – even if you feel the question is too basic or trivial. Remember that the staff who work in record offices are only there because people like you and me want to use and understand the records in their care.

If you're travelling a long distance to get to the record office, particularly if you're not expecting to be able to go back regularly, you should do everything you can to ensure that you get the most out of your visit. Have a clear plan of what you want to achieve; make a list of the documents you want to see and find out what other records you might be able to look at while you're there.

The best source of all this information is the archive's own websites. Most record offices have very helpful sites and many of them have started to put catalogues or indexes to their most important records online. The ARCHON directory at www.nationalarchives.gov.uk/archon provides the contact details of all the record repositories in the UK and includes links to their own websites.

The more preparation you do, the more successful your day is likely to be. So don't get caught out – be prepared, and make the most of your day.

Page from the Army List, showing Lieutenant Leonard Darwin (Charles Darwin's son) of the Royal Engineers, 1873–75.

Chapter 9

For Queen, King and Country: Military service records

The British Army
Militia and volunteer forces
The Royal Navy
The Royal Marines
The Royal Air Force
The Merchant Navy

At its height, the British Empire covered nearly a quarter of the earth's land surface and encompassed almost one fifth of the world's population. From the late 16th century until the mid 1900s, England (and later the Kingdom of Great Britain and the UK) had commercial interests in just about every corner of the globe: from Australia to Central America, from Africa to South East Asia and of course, most significantly, across the whole of the Indian sub-continent.

Defending these commercial interests in the far-flung outposts of the British Empire became an increasingly important task as the empire continued to grow throughout the 18th and 19th centuries. The role of protecting this vast empire (so large that it was said that the sun never set on it) fell to those two illustrious branches of the British military machine: the Army and the Royal Navy. Their aggressive and unrelenting recruitment policy had a huge impact on the lives of ordinary people, the length and breadth of the British Isles and for the first time in British history, large numbers of men (some with their families in tow) left these shores: their job, to deal with the threats posed by rival colonial powers and to quell local uprisings.

Exactly how many men have ever served in the British Army or the Royal Navy over the centuries is impossible to calculate, but it's fair to say that the military forces have always been one of the UK's largest employers. We know that during the Napoleonic era there were more than 250,000 men on the Army's books and that in 1861, following the merging of the East India Company's forces in India with the standing British Army, approximately 220,000 soldiers were listed on the regimental muster rolls. At the height of the Boer War, the 1901 census report stated that 'the entire Army' then comprised 441,935 officers and men (at home and abroad) while there were 90,559 men recorded as serving in the Royal Navy. During the First World War, the regular Army's ranks were swelled by volunteers and conscripts to around five million men with an additional 600,000 seeing service in the Navy.

So there's a very good chance that somewhere in your family tree you will have a relative who saw active service with one branch or another of Britain's military forces. The documents recording their service have largely found their way into the holdings of The National Archives and large swathes of them are now available online.

The British Army

The history of the British Army as we know it today began when the crowns of England and Scotland were formally united in 1707 and the countries' two armies became one. The British Army was administered from London by the War Office and the records of this government department form one of the largest collections held by The National Archives today: 415 distinct series of records comprising over half a million archival 'pieces' and an incalculable number of discrete documents. The majority of the records relate to the administration and operation of the Army, but a significant part of the collection refers directly to individual officers and men, and it's these records which family historians can use to research the careers of their military ancestors.

Regimental musters survive from around 1730 so it's sometimes possible to trace an individual's army service from a very early date. However, the earliest formal service records (usually in the form of documents recording the award of an Army pension) only exist from about 1760, while discharge papers don't start until 1817. Records of medal awards from 1793, certificates of service from the 1780s, description books from 1756 and records of deserters (which survive well from the first half of the 19th century) can all help to tell the fascinating story of an individual soldier's military career.

Some of the earliest surviving records, starting in 1702, relate to muster rolls of Pensioners admitted to the Royal Hospital at Chelsea but generally speaking, it's easier to trace a 19th-century soldier through the surviving records than one who served earlier or later.

The General Register Office holds a large collection of Army birth, baptism, marriage and death registers which will be dealt with in Chapter 12.

The records of our army ancestors at The National Archives are distributed among a wide range of War Office record series and many of them are beyond the scope of this book. Some of the records relating to the Royal Engineers and Royal Artillery are in separate series as are records of the Militia and other volunteer forces.

In most cases, there are separate records for officers and 'men' – i.e. ordinary soldiers such as privates, corporals and sergeants in the infantry regiments and troopers in the cavalry.

Pension and service records

There were two basic types of British Army pensions: in-pensions, paid to men who were no longer fit for service and literally 'hospitalised'; and out-pensions, awarded to men who had been discharged after completing their allotted number of years, or as a result of wounds or sickness suffered 'in the service'.

It's important to note that not everyone who served in the British Army received a pension. You won't generally find service records for men who were dishonourably discharged or who died in service.

In order to assess a man's entitlement to pension, the Royal Hospital at Chelsea used the attestation and discharge documents created and compiled by the soldier's regiment. The Royal Hospital in Kilmainham (Dublin) performed the same role for Irish soldiers until 1822. And it's not hard to appreciate the value of these records to family historians.

Collectively known as the Soldiers' Documents, they provide information about a soldier's age, place of birth and trade at the time of his enlistment, along with a physical description – height, weight, chest measurement, complexion, colour of eyes and hair and any distinguishing features, such as scars and tattoos. In an era before photography, this was vital information for an organisation which was rightly concerned about its capacity to identify, recapture and, ultimately, punish deserters.

From the mid to late 19th century, attestation papers often record information about the soldier's next of kin – specifically their name and address – which, since the forms were working documents, were frequently updated as a soldier's circumstances changed. For example, when a man got married, his wife rather than his father or mother became his legal next of kin – and this should be indicated on his attestation form. Similarly, the death of a parent may result in a change being recorded.

These later attestation forms also have a section to record detailed information about the soldier's marriage (his wife's name and the date and place of marriage) together with the particulars of any children (names, dates and places of birth and baptism). Awards of campaign or long-service medals, details of educational qualifications and the dates of promotions and reductions in rank should all be recorded on attestation forms.

The Soldiers' Documents can also include any number of sheets recording additional details, such as a soldier's medical history and, perhaps surprisingly frequently, signed declarations that a soldier had enlisted under a false name. All of this is clearly of huge interest to family historians.

The records (covering service from 1760 to 1913) are held by The National Archives in record series WO 97 (WO 96 for the Militia) and the entire collection is now available online on the FindMyPast website, making access to these fascinating documents easier than ever before.

The National Archives holds a separate collection of 'Certificates of Service' in record series WO 121, covering men who were discharged to out-pensions between 1787 and 1813. Similar certificates issued to men who were awarded deferred pensions between 1838 and 1896 are in record series WO 131 and there are many other potentially useful 'service' records in other series, such as WO 25, WO 116, WO 117 and WO 120.

Muster rolls and pay lists

The Army's muster rolls and pay lists record the state of a regiment or battalion at a given time. Each discrete document comprises the musters for a single year (usually from April to March) and, as The

National Archives holds over 70,000 muster rolls, we are clearly dealing with an exceptionally large collection of material.

Musters were taken at regular monthly or quarterly intervals and list the names of the officers and men on the regiment's 'strength'. The musters record the regiment's current location and also provide details of the rates of pay for individual soldiers, along with any deductions for disciplinary matters and additional payments for 'Good Conduct' awards. When a soldier joined the regiment and at the time of his discharge, additional biographical information can sometimes be found, including details of his age, place of birth, next of kin and trade. If a soldier was transferred to another regiment this will be recorded in the muster rolls, as will details of any overseas service. By following a soldier through successive muster rolls you should be able to build up a detailed picture of his time with the regiment – and since many men served for a full 21 years, this can represent a considerable amount of data.

At the time of writing none of the actual documents are available online, but the FindMyPast website includes an invaluable index to the muster rolls for the whole of the British Army for the year 1861.

Medals
Whether awarded for long service, for specific campaigns or for gallantry or meritorious service, the records of our ancestors' military decorations can be of enormous benefit to family historians as we attempt to piece together the details of their army careers. They can be particularly useful if the person you're looking for wasn't discharged to pension, as they will enable you to identify the soldier's regiment, which in turn will lead you to the relevant muster rolls.

The records of all Campaign Medals awarded from 1793 onwards are listed in a series of registers held by The National Archives in record series WO 100. Although the Waterloo medal was the first to be awarded, the Military General Service Medal (awarded retrospectively in 1847 to survivors of the Napoleonic conflict) predates it by 22 years as far as service is concerned.

From the Peninsular War to the Crimea; the Indian Mutiny and the Afghan campaign; Egypt and the Sudan; Burma and China; Somaliland and the various South African wars, the medal rolls represent a potted history of the British Army in the volatile 19th century.

The records extend well into the 20th century – there are registers for the General Service Medal (1918-1962) and the Indian General Service Medals (1908-1939).

The complete collection of 'Campaign Medal and Award Rolls' is now available online on the Ancestry website. These records do not include awards of medals for service during the First World War (see below).

Awards for gallantry have been made in times of war (as well as peace) since the Middle Ages, but for our purposes the idea of a medal for meritorious service was first conceived in 1854 with the establishment of the Distinguished Conduct Medal (DCM), followed two years later by the Victoria Cross (VC).

The next major award to be instituted was the Distinguished Service Order (DSO) in 1886, and the First World War saw the introduction of the Military Cross (MC) and the Military Medal (MM). The records of the awards of these medals are spread over a number of TNA record series, notably WO 98, WO 373, WO 390 and WO 391.

WO 101 comprises a series of registers recording Meritorious Service Awards between 1846 and 1919.

Announcements of almost all of these awards were made in the London Gazette (the government's official newspaper) which is fully searchable online at www.london-gazette.co.uk. Records of Recommendations for Honours and Awards (1935-1990) are searchable on The National Archives' Discovery website and the Victoria Cross Registers.

The Long Service and Good Conduct Medal was instituted in 1833 and the records of the award of this medal are held by The National Archives in record series WO 102. These records can be browsed as 'digital microfilm' on www.nationalarchives.gov.uk/records/digital-microfilm.htm.

The First World War and beyond

The 'War To End All Wars' touched the lives of ordinary families throughout the British Isles in a way that no other conflict had done before and no other has since. Of the five million men who saw active service (mainly in the trenches on the Western Front or as part of the ill-fated Gallipoli campaign) nearly one in five (almost one million) failed to return home. Another 1.6 million men were wounded in the conflict, meaning that around five per cent of the UK's population was directly affected. It's easy to see that very few UK families would have escaped the devastating consequences of the war and anecdotal evidence appears to bear this out. Even if a family didn't lose a loved son themselves, the chances are that their neighbours did. Research has shown that only 52 villages in the whole of the UK survived the war without suffering any casualties – these so called 'Thankful' villages (there are none in Scotland or Ireland) are the fortunate few.

In the light of this unprecedented carnage it would seem somewhat insensitive to describe the loss of 60 per cent of the British Army's First World War service records as a tragedy. But for family historians, the loss leaves us with a considerable gap in the story of our recent ancestors' lives. Ironically, the records were destroyed as the result of an enemy attack during the Second World War, when an incendiary device struck the London repository where they were being stored.

The surviving files (many of which were further damaged by the water used to control the fire caused by the bomb) have been supplemented by a collection of records relating to soldiers who were discharged during the war on medical grounds and to regular soldiers (i.e. not volunteers or conscripts) who had completed their term of service. The National Archives holds microfilm copies of the two sets of records in series WO 363 and WO 364.

The records are broadly similar to the earlier service records described above and largely consist of copies of attestation and discharge papers. They can also include medical records and large numbers of forms relating to the awards and payments of pensions. The entire collection of more than 2.5 million records is fully searchable on the Ancestry website.

Information about the million or so men who died in the conflict can be found on two important databases. Soldiers Who Died In The Great War was originally published by His Majesty's Stationery Office (HMSO) in 1921 and includes the details of more than 700,000 individuals. The soldier's name, rank and regiment are listed along with his place of birth, date of death, and place of enlistment. This database is available on the Ancestry website.

A more comprehensive record of the men who lost their lives is the Commonwealth War Graves Commission's casualty database (www. cwgc.org/search-for-war-dead.aspx). This provides much of the same information as the Soldiers Who Died In The Great War database, but also frequently includes next of kin details. The database also covers deaths in the Second World War and includes details of the 67,000 civilians who were killed as a result of enemy action in the Second World War.

Campaign medals were awarded to every man who saw active service during the First World War. The records of the awards of the 1914 Star, the 1914/15 Star, the British War Medal and the Victory Medal are held by The National Archives in record series WO 329 (Service Medal and Award Rolls, First World War), along with records of the Territorial Force Medal and the Silver War Badge (awarded to people who had been discharged as physically unfit for service). The index to these records (in the form of a vast collection of index cards) is available online at The National Archives' website and on Ancestry. The index cards contain much the same information as the Medal Rolls themselves and in most cases the only additional information to be gained from the rolls is the identity of the individual battalion or unit with which the soldier served.

This piece of information is essential for a successful search in another major source for First World War family history: the War Diaries. Each unit kept a daily record of its activities throughout the period of the war and although it is exceptionally rare for individual men to be named in the diaries, the detailed information about the battalion's movements, particularly on days when the unit was under fire or engaged in direct military action, can make fascinating reading. Some of the First World War Diaries (held by The National Archives in record series WO 95) are available on The National Archives' website, but most are only available to view as original documents at Kew.

The service records of men who were still in service in 1920, and of those who joined after that date, are still held by the Ministry of Defence. The MoD will provide copies to the person themselves or (if they are dead) to their next of kin, on payment of a fee. Details of this service are available at www.veterans-uk.info/service_records/army.html.

If you know the name of the battalion or division in which an ancestor served during the Second World War, it should be possible to identify the relevant War Diaries. As with the records from the 1914–1918 war, these documents contain detailed information about the day-to-day activities of the individual army units.

One significant collection of records which is *not* held by The National Archives is a set of soldiers' effects ledgers dating from 1901 to 1960. The records relate to money owed to soldiers who died in service and usually provide the full name, regimental number, date and place of death and, crucially, details of the next of kin. The ledgers are held by the National Army Museum in London.

Army officers

The best way to begin a search for your Army officer ancestor is to use the Army Lists, published annually since 1754. These volumes list, regiment by regiment, the names of all serving officers together with their 'seniority' i.e. the date on which they were promoted from one rank to another. From 1766 the Army Lists are indexed, and by consulting a succession of lists it should quickly be possible to construct a basic beginning-to-end service record for any British Army officer. The annual lists continued until 1879, when they were replaced by quarterly lists.

Copies of the Army Lists from 1754 to 1879 can be browsed free of charge as 'digital microfilm' on The National Archives' website at http://www.nationalarchives.gov.uk/records/digital-microfilm.htm.

Officers' service records survive in a number of record series at The National Archives. The main series of records were maintained by individual regimental record offices and can now be found in WO 25 and WO 76. During the 19th century, the War Office compiled five batches of 'service statements' which now form part of record series WO 25.

As a rule, officers' service records tend to be more informative than the equivalent records for ordinary soldiers. When you add in the information to be obtained from records of the purchase of commissions (WO 31), officers' half-pay (WO 23 and PMG 4) and pensions (various series), it's usually possible to draw up a fairly complete picture of an officer's career.

Under the terms of the Test and Corporation Acts (see Chapter 8), all Army officers had to produce a record of baptism in the Church of England. The National Archives holds two collections of baptismal certificates of Army officers: one in record series WO 32 covering the years 1777 to 1868 and another in WO 42 with a broader range of years from 1755 to 1908. The latter also includes a number of marriage certificates.

Further records of officers' marriages can be found in WO 25 along with large collections of material relating to the issuing of widows' pensions. It wasn't until 1871 that officers could be awarded pensions themselves – before that, the half-pay system was used to support officers who had been wounded or whose units had been disbanded in times of peace. However, the system was heavily abused and it was quite possible for an officer to have a long Army career without actually experiencing military service of any kind.

The range and variety of documents relating to Army officers is extraordinary. Unfortunately, they are spread across a number of different record series and very few are available online. Instead, you will need to visit Kew and investigate the wealth of material hidden away in the War Office records – you would be well advised to start with the records in WO 25, a catch-all series covering a wealth of material, as set out in its catalogue description:

'...commissions and other appointments, records of service and other service matters; embarkation, disembarkation, casualty and deserter information; pay, pensions, absences and discharges; establishments; and the Militia, Army Reserve, defence of Ireland and School of Military Engineering.'

Militia and volunteer forces

The Militia has existed as a military force since 1757 when volunteer units were established throughout the country. The aim was to provide a well-trained reserve force to counter the threat of enemy invasion. Conscripts could also be selected by ballot to serve in the various County Militias. The history of Britain's auxiliary forces (encompassing the Yeomanry, the Volunteers, the Special Reserve, the Territorial Force and the Home Guard, among others) is long and complicated, but since large numbers of ordinary men saw service in one or other of these volunteer forces, it's well worth investigating the surviving records. Particularly as the most important service records (the Militia attestation papers held by The National Archives in record series WO 96) are included in the main British Army Service Records database on the FindMyPast website.

The National Archives also holds a large collection of Militia description and enrolment books, mainly in record series WO 68, and there are muster rolls in WO 13. Other potentially useful records are held by local county record offices.

The Royal Navy

The history of Britain's 'senior' service can be traced back to early medieval times, but it wasn't until the reign of King Henry VIII that a 'standing' navy was first established. As the empire expanded, and the need for quick and effective communication between London and the colonies and trading outposts increased, the development of a professional sea force became a necessity, and from the late 17th century until the Seconed World War the Royal Navy, administered from London by the Admiralty, quite literally ruled the waves.

It's perhaps surprising therefore that it wasn't until 1854 that the Royal Navy introduced 'continuous' service. Before that date, ordinary sailors (known as 'ratings') were engaged for limited periods and then discharged at the end of the ship's voyage.

Recruiting ratings was always a struggle for the naval authorities: a situation which gave rise to the dreaded press gangs. Men could quite legitimately be taken from their homes (or more commonly from inns and ale houses) and 'pressed' into service. Many never returned to their families or only did so many years later.

Tracing the record of a rating in the period before continuous service can be very difficult. The main source of information is the Royal Navy's pay lists and musters (ADM 31–ADM 39, ADM 115, ADM 117 and ADM 119), which operated on much the same lines as the Army's muster rolls. The main challenge to the researcher is one of getting in to the records, as you need to know the name of the ship on which an ancestor served before you can really start.

You might get this information from a medal award. The Royal Navy kept records of the awards of various medals, and registers covering the years 1793 to 1972 (held by The National Archives in record series ADM 171) are available on the Ancestry website. The records usually show the name of the ship on which the recipient of the medal served.

Once you've been able to track down an ancestor to a particular ship it should, in theory at least, be possible to trace their service backwards and forwards through the records. The name of the rating's previous ship should be recorded when they first appear on the pay lists, and the method of discharge should similarly include the name of the ship to which they were 'transferred'. However, it's not always as easy as this, as the record-keeping was not always as efficient as we would like.

The muster rolls and pay lists will also give you details of the ship's voyages, which can be supplemented by information from the ship's log books.

Full service records, covering men who saw service in the Royal Navy between 1854 and 1923, are held by The National Archives in record series ADM 139 and ADM 188 digitised and indexed online at http://www.nationalarchives.gov.uk/records/royal-naval-seamen. htm. The records usually consist of a single pre-printed form containing the rating's name, date and place of birth and date of engagement, along with a brief physical description.

The main body of the form comprises a list of the 'Ships served in' which includes the periods of service on board the various vessels, dates of promotion through the ranks, awards of any Good Conduct medals and observations as to the rating's character. The date and cause of discharge should also be recorded together with details of any campaign or gallantry medals awarded.

Some of the details are heavily abbreviated and can be quite difficult to interpret, and the records seem quite sparse when compared to the much fuller Army records – there is, for example, rarely any reference to other family members – but the information is generally useful and it all helps to piece together your naval ancestor's life story.

A word of warning: the dates of birth in these records are notoriously inaccurate!

The Royal Greenwich Hospital performed the same role for the Royal Navy and its men as the hospitals at Chelsea and Kilmainham did for the Army. Pensioners' admission papers and entry books (in ADM 73) and Certificates of Service (in ADM 29) can provide invaluable information about an ancestor's naval career and can lead you back into the period before the introduction of continuous service. These records are indexed and the main details can be accessed via The National Archives' online catalogue. The catalogue will provide you with the relevant archival reference to allow you to view the original document at Kew. Earlier pension records can be found in record series ADM 6, ADM 22 and ADM 73.

Records of men whose service began after 1923 are still held by the Ministry of Defence. Access to the records is restricted to the person themselves or their next of kin. Details can be found at www.veterans-uk.info/service_records/royal_navy.html.

Naval officers

Published quarterly since 1782, the Navy List will provide you with the basic outline of a Royal Naval officer's career. The lists give the names of the serving officers, their rank and seniority and the name of the ship in which they were then serving.

Officers' service records survive in the form of registers compiled by the Admiralty from the 1840s onwards and held by The National Archives in record series ADM 196. The registers include records of service dating back as far as the late 18th century, but the earlier records are known to be incomplete.

The Admiralty also conducted a number of 'service surveys' during the 19th century in which serving and retired officers were asked to provide details of their naval service. The surveys are far from being comprehensive but should one survive for your ancestor, it would naturally be of great interest. The surviving records are held in a variety of series – ADM 6, ADM 9, ADM 10 and ADM 11. As with the other naval service records, these surveys rarely contain much information of a genealogical nature, as family details were not requested. The service registers and the surveys are all searchable on The National Archives' website.

One final source which is worth considering in the search for your naval officer ancestors is the officer's Passing Certificates. Many naval officers had to sit an exam before they could be 'passed' as suitable for promotion to a higher rank; the certificates recording this process are held by The National Archives in record series ADM 6, ADM 13, ADM 106 and ADM 107. Possibly the most significant collection is the Lieutenant's Passing Certificates (1691–1902) which have been fully indexed by name and published by the List and Index Society (volumes 289 and 290).

The Royal Marines

The Royal Marines were established in 1755, although the history of the force can be traced back to 1664 when the Duke of York and Albany's Maritime Regiment of Foot was first recruited. The idea of an armed fighting force which would be based onboard Royal Naval vessels became a vital cog in the British military machine and the Marines have played an important role in every major conflict involving British forces in the past 300 years.

Administratively speaking the Royal Marines are a part of the Royal Navy, but the Admiralty have always kept separate records for the two forces. For most of its history, the Royal Marines operated three 'Grand

Divisions', based at Chatham, Plymouth and Portsmouth. A further division was established at Woolwich between 1805 and 1869.

As far as service records are concerned, the Royal Marines are well covered. Attestation forms (in ADM 157) survive from as early as 1790 for the Chatham Division. Some of these records have been indexed and can be accessed via The National Archives' online catalogue digitised and indexed at http://www.nationalarchives.gov.uk/records/marines.htm. Description Books (ADM 158) start even earlier, with some extending back as far as the initial establishment of the Royal Marines in 1755.

The main series of service records consists of bound registers containing pre-printed forms, very similar in nature to the Continuous Service registers produced by the Royal Navy. These will tell you the name, date and place of birth and previous trade of each man, along with the usual physical description. The date and place of enlistment are given, as well as details of the man's service with different companies and divisions, and the names of the ships on which he served. The date and cause of discharge, details of medals awarded and references to the man's character should also be recorded.

Service records for men who enlisted in the Royal Marines after 1925 are held by the Historical Records Office Royal Marines, Room 038, Centurion Building, Grange Road, Gosport, Hampshire PO13 9XA.

The Royal Air Force

The RAF was formed on 1 April 1918 when the aeronautical wings of the British Army (the Royal Flying Corps) and the Royal Navy (the Royal Naval Air Service) were amalgamated. At the time of writing, only a small percentage of the records relating to the Royal Air Force are publicly available.

The records of approximately 330,000 men who served in the RAF during the First World War and were discharged before 1922 are held by The National Archives (in record series AIR 79). The records, which are now searchable (by name only) on The National Archives' online catalogue, can be very informative. The airman's full name, date and place of birth, date of entry into the service and civilian occupation are all given, along with details of his marriage, next of kin and the names of any children. The main body of the form has space to record the airman's various postings and promotions while on the reverse there's room for comments about his character, any special qualifications and

– of particular importance since there is no separate First World War medal roll for the RAF – a space to record any 'casualties, wounds, campaigns, medals, clasps, decorations, mentions etc'.

Service records for airmen who were discharged after 1922 are still held by the Royal Air Force. Details of how to apply for copies of these can be found at www.veterans-uk.info/service_records/raf.html.

The Air Ministry combat reports (covering the years 1939–1945) are available on The National Archives' website and can be searched by squadron or surname. The records can provide fascinating details of an airman's experiences during the Second World War.

RAF officers' service records covering the years 1918–1922 are available on The National Archives' website.

The Merchant Navy

Although not strictly speaking a military force, the service provided by the Merchant Navy in the two World Wars was of such importance to the war efforts that a brief mention of the surviving service records warrants inclusion here.

As there was no continuous service in the Royal Navy before 1854, men could, and frequently did, move between ships of the Royal Navy and merchant vessels during the 19th century and before then. Indeed, merchant sailors would have been at the top of the list for any press gang seeking suitable fresh 'recruits'.

Recognising the problem, the Merchant Shipping Act of 1835 introduced a form of registration for merchant seamen which would provide the Royal Navy with the necessary information to create a reserve force in times of war. The registration system went through a number of iterations before being abandoned in 1857, but it left behind an enormous amount of paperwork.

The Board of Trade oversaw the creation of three Seamen's Registers (Series I covering the years 1835–1836; Series II from 1835–1844; and Series III from 1853–1857) which were interrupted by the introduction of a ticketing system lasting from 1845–1855. The records of these registers and tickets are held by The National Archives in record series BT 112–114, BT 116 and BT 119–120.

For the next 56 years, the Board of Trade operated without a centralised registration system, arguing that the Crew Lists and Agreements (see below) provided sufficient information for their administrative purposes, but in 1913 a Fourth Register was opened (BT 348–350). Unfortunately, the records covering the years 1913–1918 were destroyed, so in reality the records start in 1919, leaving a 62-year gap in the records.

The records of the four registers and the seamen's tickets have all been digitised and indexed and are available to search on the FindMyPast website.

In 1941 a Fifth Register was opened. Records of men who were in the service in 1941 were carried forward from the Fourth Register, so if your ancestor's service continued into the Second World War and beyond you would expect to find his service record in this later Register. The records are in a variety of record series (BT 364, BT 372 and BT 382) and are subject to data protection restrictions.

The Board of Trade also kept separate records of Merchant Navy officers, including a Register of Masters (1845–1854) in record series BT 115 and a set of registers of Certificates of Competency and Service for the years 1845 to 1921 (BT 122–130 and BT 139–142). These include details of masters, mates, engineers and skippers of fishing boats.

Crew Lists and Agreements have been kept since the middle of the 18th century, but only survive in significant numbers from the early 1800s. As with the Royal Naval musters and pay lists, in theory it is possible to trace a man's career from ship to ship using the information recorded in these documents, but the reality is that the standards of record-keeping are not always good enough to allow this. The surviving records are held by The National Archives in record series BT 98–100.

The records of more than 100,000 medals issued to merchant seamen for service during the Second World War can be searched on The National Archives' website. The records (in BT 395) record the full name of the seaman as well as any medals, ribbons and clasps to which he was entitled, and usually include his date and place of birth. The National Archives also provides searchable online access to Merchant seamen's campaign medal records 1914–1918 (in BT 351 and MT 9).

Less is more

The digital age has led to many changes in the way that we go about researching the lives of our ancestors, and the successful family historian has had to learn a number of new skills.

A basic understanding of how databases work has now become an essential tool in the 21st-century researcher's locker. The ability to interrogate a database effectively can make all the difference between a positive search and that bane of the family historian – the 'no results' screen.

Most of the websites that we use have broadly similar search screens. We're all used to the basic layout: a series of labelled boxes (or fields), some containing drop-down menus, others inviting you to enter a name, a date or an age. The temptation for the inexperienced searcher is to complete all the boxes: the logic would seem to be that the more information you supply about your ancestor, the more chance you have of finding them. But in fact, to a degree at least, the opposite is true.

When we enter data into the fields on a search screen we are effectively applying a filter to the database. We're asking the computer to show us all the records in the data set that match the details that we're looking for. In most cases, what we'll get are exact matches – and if just one of the pieces of data that we've entered fails to match the relevant piece of data in the database, the record will be filtered out and it won't appear in our results list.

But what if the information in the database was 'wrong' – either through mistranscription or because of an error in the original data? Then, the only way we're going to find the record that we're looking for is by leaving out that piece of information from our search and using other fields to produce the matches. It's a process or trial and error, but it's also about developing an understanding of which are the best fields for our search. As a general rule, first names and ages are the most likely to produce results. Surnames are too open to misinterpretation and places of birth are often too vague. If your initial search fails, don't assume that the record you're looking for isn't there. Instead, go back and search again using a different combination of fields. And if that doesn't work, try something else. The crucial thing to remember here is that less is more.

As computer systems become more sophisticated, databases are increasingly intelligent. Many will now routinely apply a form of 'fuzzy' searching. The FamilySearch website, for example, will take your search for the first name William and automatically return records with variant spellings of the name, including common abbreviations such as Wm. and Willm., as well as Latin forms, such as Guilielmus.

There are clearly advantages to this approach, but there's also a danger that the developers are producing systems that are too clever – systems that try to do our thinking for us. And it's important that we retain the ability to keep control of our searches. The human eye (ably supported by the human brain) is a far better tool than any computer when it comes to picking out the most promising candidate from a list of names.

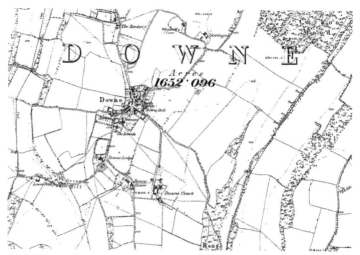

*An 1851 map of Downe, in Kent. Downe (or Down) House and its estate,
Charles Darwin's residence from the 1840s until his death, is shown to the south of
the village itself.*

Chapter 10

Picture this:
The visual dimension

Maps
Prints and photographs

Maps and photographs are among the most important sources available to family historians, yet they are also among the most frequently ignored.

Maps

Maps come in all shapes and sizes and have been produced for a huge variety of reasons over the centuries but there is no single centralised collection of maps and there is no definitive list of what exists. Maps can be found in the records of countless government departments and regularly crop up in bundles of legal documents, in the records of ecclesiastical and manorial courts and even among wills and census returns. Estate maps, transport maps showing roads, canals or railways, topographical maps and, of course, the extensive and varied collection of plans published by the Ordnance Survey will all help you to place your ancestors' lives in their geographical context.

The National Archives holds two collections of maps which are of particular value to family historians; both cover the whole of England and Wales. The earlier of them is the vast series of maps created by the Tithe Commission, which began work in 1836. The maps are accompanied by a series of 'apportionments', which are large, unwieldy documents that set out the names of the landowners and occupiers in each tithe district. They also record details of the various parcels of land, each of which is individually numbered, and it is these numbers which provide a link to the accompanying map and enable us to identify the whereabouts of the land and buildings owned or occupied by our ancestors.

Since most of the tithe maps date from around 1840, there is an obvious tie-in here with the 1841 census returns. Once you've found your ancestors in the census, a search of the relevant tithe documents should reveal exactly where they were living. In addition to the (almost) complete collection held by The National Archives, you should find that most county record offices hold tithe records for their own area.

The other significant collection of maps held by The National Archives was created by the Valuation Office under the Finance Act (1909–10). The arrangement of the documents is very similar to that used by the Tithe Commission some 70 years earlier. A series of 'field books' is linked to thousands of heavily annotated maps of various scales. The scale of the map depended on the type of district being surveyed, with large-scale maps for the larger towns and cities and smaller scales for the rural areas.

As with the tithe apportionments, the field books contain details of the individual pieces of land. They also show the names of the occupiers and owners of the land as well as information about their liability for rates and taxes. Occasionally, sketch plans of individual properties are included. The records of this survey, commonly known as Lloyd George's Domesday, are roughly contemporary with the 1911 census and so provide an excellent opportunity for us to expand our knowledge of our Edwardian ancestors.

The National Archives has developed a Valuation Office map finder at http://labs.nationalarchives.gov.uk/wordpress/index.php/2010/04/valuation-office-map-finder/.

Maps are a great way to understand how your ancestors' lives were affected and influenced by the areas in which they lived. That ancestor of yours from the small Suffolk coastal village would have led a very different sort of existence to the family who lived on the North Yorkshire moors or in the valleys of South Wales. And the lives of the inhabitants of that remote hamlet on the edge of Dartmoor would have been poles apart from those of the family who lived in the little market town lying on the main road from London to Nottingham. It's only by looking at contemporary maps of the areas that your ancestors lived in that you'll get a real feeling for all of this. The 1834 topographical maps published in *The Phillimore Atlas & Index of Parish Registers* are particularly useful, as they show the country as it was just before the process of urbanisation had really taken hold: a time when most of our ancestors still lived in rural areas. You can see at a glance whether your family's village was situated near a principal road; you can quickly identify the nearest major town – and don't ignore the waterways: rivers and canals were vital trade routes before the coming of the railways. And remember that your ancestors wouldn't have worried too much about county boundaries – it's not as if the borders were marked by fences and walls and patrolled by armed guards! So if your family lived near the edge of a county, don't forget to have a look at maps of the neighbouring areas.

Large-scale maps of the major towns and cities can help you to pinpoint the various addresses you've found in the census returns. And you can also use the maps to learn more about the areas where your ancestors lived. You can find the local churches and schools, the parks and cemeteries, the railway stations and tram routes, the factories and warehouses. The more detailed maps, showing the individual houses and gardens, will give you a good idea of the relative wealth of the area; large villas set in extensive gardens give a very different picture from the rows upon rows of terraced houses with their cramped backyards.

A Vision of Britain Through Time (http://vision.port.ac.uk) provides access to a range of maps from the 19th and early 20th centuries, along with a huge amount of topographical and statistical information about the towns and villages where our ancestors lived out their lives. Other useful websites for old maps are Old Maps Online (www. oldmapsonline.org), Cassini Historical Maps (www.cassinimaps.co. uk) and, for Scotland, the National Library of Scotland's online map library (maps.nls.uk).

The British Library, Oxford's Bodleian Library and the National Libraries of Scotland and Wales all hold their own important collections of maps.

DID YOU KNOW?

Until fairly recent times, the terms 'son-in-law' and 'daughter-in-law' were used where today we would say 'step-son' or 'step-daughter'. If you find someone described in the census as the 'son-in-law' of the head of the household, he could either be the daughter's husband or the wife's son from a previous marriage.

Prints and photographs

'What is the use of a book,' thought Alice, 'without pictures?' And the same is true of your research – after all, what is the use of a family history without pictures?

Wherever you find maps, you're also likely to find collections of prints, engravings and photographs. County record offices and local studies libraries often have large collections of visual material which you can use to illustrate your research and add an extra dimension to the story of your family.

With a bit of luck you might come across a photograph of the street that your ancestors lived in a hundred years ago. If not, then a view of the local high street will give you an idea of what the town was like, and if you discover nothing else you should at the very least be able to find an old print of the church where your great-great-grandparents were married. Most record offices will allow you to get copies from items in their photographic collections (for a fee) but don't forget to consider the copyright implications.

Old postcards are another way to illustrate your family's story. There are many companies specialising in this area, and you'll often find them at family history fairs fighting for space with the local record offices and family history society stalls. You can also find hundreds of postcards for sale on websites such as eBay.

Francis Frith was a pioneer of Victorian photography. Setting up business in Reigate in 1859, he embarked on an ambitious project to photograph every town and village in the UK. The results of his work were published as picture postcards and many of his photos are now available on a commercial website: www.francisfrith.com.

As the repository for the official copyright records of the Stationers' Company, The National Archives holds a surprisingly large collection of photographs. Record series COPY 1 comprises thousands of photographs taken between 1862 and 1912. The accompanying descriptions have been catalogued and can be searched on The National Archives' online catalogue by keywords.

Another large collection of photographs held by The National Archives is the Dixon-Scott Collection. Taken during the 1920s and 1930s by J Dixon-Scott, the photographs cover the whole of the British Isles and can be searched by place name at TNA Labs http://labs.national archives. gov.uk/wordpress/.

If you're thinking of publishing your family history (in printed form or on the Internet) or if you just want to get a bit of additional background for your own personal interest, a good selection of prints and photographs, together with some photos from your own family albums, will add a whole new dimension and really bring your research to life.

Putting flesh on the bones

The results of your family history research should be so much more than a long list of names and dates. Of course you need to do all the basics; you need to discover your ancestors' dates of birth, marriage and death and you need to know when their children were born, but ideally the discovery of these facts should be a means to an end.

As a family historian you should look at as diverse a range of sources as possible – particularly those that are traditionally thought of as sources for local history. In order to understand them better, you need to find out more about the areas that your people came from. What were the main trades and industries? Who were the chief landowners and how did they influence your ancestors' lives? Was the population of the town on the increase or was it declining? When did the railways arrive and what effect did this have on the town?

The chances are that the answers to these questions have already been researched and published. There can't be a town or city in England and Wales which hasn't been the subject of at least one major historical study, and you'll probably find that several have been published over the years. Even quite small villages are likely to have something on offer.

Local studies libraries are an excellent source for this sort of material, and you should also find that they have good collections of earlier county histories in which 18th- and 19th-century historians looked at the history of their counties from the perspective of the major landowners. Although these might seem to have little relevance to those of us with ancestors who worked on the land rather than owned it, it's always worthwhile finding out what they have to say about your ancestors' parish – you never know what you might discover.

Social, political and even national history are also areas that you should investigate. Your ancestors may not have taken part in the Captain Swing Riots of 1830 and they may not have been among the crowd at St Peter's Field, Manchester in 1819 to witness the Peterloo Massacre, but if they lived through these times they would certainly have been affected by the events. If any of your ancestors were agricultural labourers living in southern England in 1830, the social and economic factors that led to the Swing Riots and the transportation of the Tolpuddle Martyrs a few years later would have been of enormous importance to them, and it's therefore likely that they would have had strong opinions on the issues of the day.

Similarly, the Chartist movement of the 1830s and 1840s had a huge impact on the lives of ordinary people. Over three million people signed a petition, which was presented to Parliament in 1842, demanding the introduction of universal male suffrage – at this stage, even most Chartists felt that votes for women was a step too far. The petition was rejected but the campaign continued, and it's not at all unlikely that your ancestors were actively involved.

The English Civil War touched the lives of practically everyone who lived in the middle of the 17th century. Again, your ancestors may not have been involved in any of the pitched battles or sieges, and they may not have had particularly strong Royalist or Parliamentarian views themselves, but they can hardly fail to have been affected by the conflict in some way or other.

The most important thing to remember here is that the names on your family tree relate to real people: people with real hopes and fears; people who would have been devastated by the early death of their youngest son just as they were overjoyed by the birth of their first grandchild; people who lived through dramatic national and local events. Foreign wars and the failure of a crop would equally have affected their lives.

So when you come across that single line in the parish register recording your ancestor's baptism, don't just make a note of the date and move quickly on to the next item on your list. Instead, try to imagine the baby wrapped in her christening robes as the vicar holds her over the font and her parents look on, happy but a little anxious. Picture the same parents twenty years on, as they proudly watch their daughter walking up the aisle to start a new life with the blacksmith's son, who they've known since *he* was a baby. And then the sad scene at the graveside in the churchyard of the same parish church as, through tear-filled eyes, the young woman sees her father's coffin lowered into the ground, with her own children gathered beside her.

Family history isn't a scientific pursuit, it's a voyage of discovery, and your aim should be to learn as much as you can about your ancestors as real people – and to find out what their lives were really like.

84 *Obituary of remarkable Persons; with Biographical Anecdotes.* **Jan.**

ther in improving the condition, or in adding to the comforts of human nature, yet she never suffered them to encroach on, or in the least degree interfere with, the indispensable duties of domestic life, to which her superintendence and care were attentively directed. The indigent and distressed have lost a kind and compassionate friend; the sympathy and benevolence of her heart ever disposed her patiently to listen to the tale of woe, and her hand was equally ready liberally to administer to its relief. To manners peculiarly attracting, were united a natural and unaffected vivacity, and sweetness of disposition, that rendered her conversation and society highly interesting to her friends and acquaintance. Farther to enlarge might have the appearance of panegyric: to say thus much is a tribute justly due to her many and amiable virtues, which never can cease to have a place in the memory of those who knew her, and were such as render her loss irreparable to an affected husband, son, and daughter. She was sister to Mr. Hill, whose Observations on France were reviewed vol. LXII. p. 361.

3. In his 84th year, Edward Sneyd, esq. formerly major in the horse guards, and many years one of his Majesty's gentlemen ushers.

At Edinburgh, Isaac Grant, esq. writer to the signet.

Mrs. Kitching, wife of Stephenson Kitching, esq. of West Ham, Essex.

Aged 60, Mrs. Haycock, a widow lady, of Stamford, after a severe illness of several years continuance, which she bore with great resignation.

The eldest son of Mr Edward Gibbons, of Claverton-Down. While shooting, his companion, firing hastily close behind him, shot him directly through the head, and literally blew it to pieces, so that he died in an instant. He was a youth of good character, an d about twenty-one years of age.

Mr. Burton, baker, of Glenfield.

Found dead in her bed, Miss Mellor, of Chesterfield.

At Etruria, in Staffordshire, aged 64, Josiah Wedgwood, esq. F.R. and A. SS; to whose indefatigable labours is owing the establishment of a manufacture that has opened a new scene of extensive commerce, before unknown to this or any other country. It is unnecessary to say that this alludes to the Pottery of Staffordshire, which, by the united efforts of Mr. Wedgwood and his late partner, Mr. Bentley, has been carried to a degree of perfection, both in the line of utility and ornament, that leaves all works, antient or modern, far behind. But, though this improvement of the manufacture in which he was bred, and which had been the employment of his family for several generations, occupied much of Mr. W's time, he was frequently employed in planning designs that will for ever record the greatness of his mind; for, however the

practicability of uniting the Eastern and Western coasts of this kingdom, by means of inland navigation, may have been shewn by Yarranton and others, yet it remained for Mr. W. to propose such measures for uniting the Duke of Bridgewater's Canal with the navigable part of the River Trent (in executing which he was happy in the assistance of the late ingenious Mr. Brindley, whom he never mentioned but with respect), as first fully carried the great plan into execution, and thus enabled the manufacturers of the inland part of that county and its neighbourhood to obtain, from the distant shores of Devonshire, Dorsetshire, and Kent, those materials of which the Staffordshire ware is composed; affording, at the same time, a ready conveyance of the manufacture to distant countries; and thus not only to rival, but undersell, at foreign markets, a commodity which has proved, and must continue to prove, of infinite advantage to these kingdoms; as the ware, when formed, owes its value almost wholly to the labour of the honest and industrious poor, who have, in Mr. W, lost a kind master and generous benefactor. Still farther to promote the interest and benefit of his neighbourhood, Mr. W. planned, and carried into execution, a turnpike-road, ten miles in length, through that part of Staffordshire called The Pottery; thus opening another source of traffick, if, by frost or other impediment, the carriage by water should be interrupted. Having given this imperfect sketch of his public life, let us consider him in his private capacity; wherein, whether he is regarded as a husband, a father, a master, or a friend, his conduct will be found most exemplary.

Such is the account of Mr. W. sent us by an old and valuable correspondent, who knew him long and intimately. Another correspondent adds, that " Mr. W. was the younger son of a potter, but derived little or no property from his father, whose possessions consisted chiefly of a small entailed estate, which descended to the eldest son. He was the maker of his own fortune: and his country has been benefited in a proportion not to be calculated. His many discoveries of new species of earthen-wares and porcelains, his studied forms and chaste style of decoration, and the correctness and judgement with which all his works were executed under his own eye, and by artists, for the most part, of his own forming, have turned the current in this branch of commerce; for, before his time, England imported the finer earthen-wares; but, for more than twenty years past, she has exported them to a very great annual amount, the whole of which is drawn from the earth, and from the industry of the inhabitants; while the national taste has been improved, and its reputation raised in foreign countries. His inventions have prodigiously increased the number of persons

Extract from The Gentleman's Magazine, January 1795, showing the opening section of an obituary of Josiah Wedgwood (1730–1795).

Chapter 11

Read all about it: Newspapers

Newspapers and family history
Newspaper collections
A magazine of note
The whole truth?

Newspapers have been with us now for over 300 years, but it wasn't until the middle of the 19th century that they really became such an important part of everyday life for most people in England and Wales. The key date is 29 June 1855, the day on which newspaper stamp duty was abolished and the era of the free press truly began. In the words of a contemporary poem, published in *The Manchester Guardian*, the passing of the Newspaper Stamp Act gave rise to 'a perfect flood of papers'.

Newspapers and family history

As a source for family history research, newspapers are unrivalled. And they all have a contribution to make to our research, from the national broadsheets like *The Times*, *The Daily Telegraph* and *The Guardian* with their comprehensive coverage of national and international events, to the early 19th century 'county' journals, which also tended to cover national news but with a slight local flavour to it. Perhaps the most important to family history are the thousands of local newspapers which appeared in the middle of the 19th century and, as the years progressed, began to focus more and more on genuinely local news. Newspapers have much to offer the family historian, but as with so many of these useful sources, if you want to get the best out of them you'll probably need to prepare yourself for a lot of long and occasionally frustrating searching.

Carrying out a speculative search in your local newspaper is unlikely to produce anything worthwhile. You really need to have the date of a specific event in mind and you need to consider whether the event is likely to have been covered by the paper. And don't forget that there may have been more than one local newspaper for your area – it was not at all uncommon to find two or more rival publications operating in the same town, often representing different political interests.

Even in Victorian times, most local newspapers provided columns where, for a small fee, people could announce the births, marriages and deaths of their nearest and dearest. While these announcements can be quite useful to us, they are unlikely to reveal anything that couldn't be discovered from other primary sources. Having said that, you may occasionally stumble across the announcement of the death of an uncle who emigrated to New Zealand 50 years ago, or the birth of a child who was previously unknown to you.

Some newspapers published quite extensive reports on local weddings, particularly if the couple getting married happened to be the children of local dignitaries. If you're lucky enough to find a report like this, you may get some very useful information from the guest lists which often accompanied the report.

It's in the areas relating to deaths that local newspapers really come into their own. The Victorian fascination with reading the reports of inquests has already been mentioned but bears repeating – they really are an important source, particularly as the original coroner's reports may have been destroyed or may still be 'closed'. Whenever you see the words 'coroner' or 'inquest' on a death certificate you should look for a report in the relevant local newspaper.

And if your ancestor was a person of any standing in the town, it is well worth checking the local newspapers for the week or two after his or her death. A good, thorough, well-researched obituary can be worth its weight in gold. You may learn when and where your ancestor was born and where he was educated; you may discover that he served in the Army and was awarded a medal for bravery; he may have been a member of the town council or a senior trade unionist, or perhaps he was a prominent local sportsman and captained the local cricket team. If you're lucky, you might even find a picture of him accompanying the report.

If you do find something like this, don't stop there. It's quite likely that the following week's paper will include a report of his funeral, together with a list of the mourners. Not only will this add to your knowledge of the family but, now that you know where he was buried, you have a whole new source to investigate.

If your ancestors were tradesmen or shopkeepers it's possible that they may have advertised their services in the local newspaper. Many of these adverts were highly decorative works of art in their own right, and for the family historian they can add an interesting visual aspect to your documentary research. Local and national newspapers regularly publish legal announcements from solicitors asking people to contact them if they believe they are related to a person who has recently died, leaving behind a substantial sum of money but no will.

The significance of this sort of announcement is obvious to family historians, but be warned that if the inspiration behind your research is the thought of discovering a long-lost family fortune you are almost certain to be disappointed!

As with the sources we looked at in the last chapter, newspapers can also be used to colour the background of your ancestors' lives. The report of a fatal accident in a mine in South Wales is the story of an event that would have affected not just the miner and his family but the whole local community. The contemporary reports of the death and funeral of Queen Victoria, for example, illustrate just how our ancestors' lives were influenced and shaped by these local and national events; and newspapers can help us to understand exactly what in these events was important to them.

Newspaper collections

The collection of the British Library's newspaper library at Colindale comprises over 50,000 titles dating from 1699 up to the present day – a total of 664,000 bound volumes and over 370,000 reels of microfilm. The bulk of the collection relates to newspapers published in the UK and the Republic of Ireland, but there are also large numbers of foreign titles, including many from Western Europe and the former British colonies. The Newspaper Library has an extensive collection of journals and periodicals so if, for example, your ancestor was involved in a trade or had an active interest in a particular sport or hobby it might be worth investigating whether there's a relevant publication that would help you to find out more about him.

In April 2012, the British Library, in association with brightsolid, launched a groundbreaking new website: the British Newspaper Archive (www.britishnewspaperarchive.co.uk). The website will eventually provide access to over 40 million pages of newsprint – already, at the time of writing, just short of six million pages have been scanned and digitised.

As part of the process, the digital images undergo an optical character recognition (OCR) process which creates electronically searchable text. The quality of this process leaves a lot to be desired but, nevertheless, the ability to search across a whole host of provincial newspapers is undeniably of major benefit to family historians.

A number of titles of national importance are already available online, notably *The Times*, which is fully searchable via the Times Digital Archive from 1785 to 2006.

Local studies libraries usually have copies of the newspapers that were published in their own areas of interest and many have collections of cuttings with card indexes.

The whole truth?

Before we leave newspapers, a word of warning. Almost all of us, at some time in our lives, will have come into contact with the local press. Perhaps you scored the winning goal for your school team or you were involved in a car accident; maybe you were a witness to a street theft or you gave a talk to your local women's group. It's a pretty safe bet that when you saw the article in the paper the following week, you found that at least one detail was incorrect or that something in the report was slightly inaccurate.

This is not intended to be a criticism of journalists, local or otherwise; after all, we already know that we shouldn't believe everything we read in the papers.

Nevertheless, as family historians it's important that we always remember this when we're reading reports of our ancestors' activities and, as with other sources that we use in the course of our research, we should always ask questions and never take 'facts' on trust.

DID YOU KNOW?

If your ancestor was a 'journeyman tailor' or a 'journeyman blacksmith', don't be fooled into thinking that this meant that he travelled around the country as part of his job. The term 'journeyman' describes someone who has served an apprenticeship in a particular trade or handicraft and is now working for someone else. His employer would be a 'master' of his trade.

Digging around

By the time you've searched all the 19th-century census returns for your ancestors' village, spent hours trawling through the parish registers and pored over an assortment of local maps, you'll start to feel that you've really got to know the place. But there's no substitute for making a personal visit to the areas that your ancestors knew so well.

If they came from a small town or village, you might be lucky and discover that not much has changed. The church is still there with the almshouses next to it; the old inn on the village green is still serving food and drink and the village store is open for business. You may even find that the house your family lived in hundreds of years ago is still standing and in good repair, and you can let yourself imagine the barefooted children running out of the back door, along the lane and across the fields.

Some of the older residents may have known your family, and if you let them know why you're visiting the village they may relish the opportunity to get talking about the past. The owner of the local store will probably be able to tell you the best people to talk to about the history of the village.

Of course, you'll want to spend some time walking around the churchyard, and naturally you'll be hoping to find some family gravestones. Take your time and look carefully at each of the stones – just as when you're looking through a parish register, you can easily miss something important if you rush these things. Strong sunlight will help you to read the more difficult inscriptions but if they're covered in moss, ivy or lichen there may be nothing you can do. You should seek permission and expert advice before attempting to clean any stones, as you can easily do more harm than good.

Some types of stone do not cope well with the wet English winters and can become badly decayed after a hundred years or so, and some may have fallen over, face down, making them impossible to read. You should never attempt to lift a fallen stone – graveyards can be dangerous places if you don't take sensible precautions. And don't forget that there may be quite recent burials next to the graves of your long-dead ancestors – think about where you're walking and treat all graves with respect and consideration.

Even in the more developed areas, there's a lot to be said for spending some time exploring the neighbourhood. The old houses may have gone and the street layout may have changed beyond recognition, but many of the features that your ancestors knew are probably still there – the churches, the parks, the schools and the town hall, for instance.

If you're spending a few days in the area, you should take the opportunity to visit the appropriate local studies library. They are often understaffed and under-resourced and their opening times may be quite limited, but they are a wonderful source, and one of the main reasons that they don't receive the funding they so badly need is that they are not used enough. Their collections of local material are unique and irreplaceable and the staff who work there probably have an expert knowledge of the area. You may have to make an appointment to use the facilities, so make sure that you plan your trip well in advance.

One of the most useful tools you can take with you on these excursions into the past is a camera. Think of it as your opportunity to make a record for future generations of what the area looked like when you went walking in your ancestors' footsteps.

A page from the registers of St Cuthbert's, Edinburgh recording the burial of Charles Darwen [sic], uncle of the scientist, Charles Darwin in 1778.

Chapter 12

The bigger picture: The British Isles

> Scotland
> Ireland
> The Channel Islands and the Isle of Man

Up to this point, this book has concerned itself largely with the records used to trace English and Welsh ancestors. In this chapter we'll take a closer look at the other parts of the British Isles.

Although the kingdoms of England and Scotland were formally unified in 1707 and the resulting Kingdom of Great Britain was later united with the Kingdom of Ireland (by the terms of the Act of Union of 1800), the kingdoms retained a degree of autonomy. The independent legal systems operating in Scotland and Ireland have led to the creation of entirely separate collections of records.

Scotland

Scottish civil registration records of births, marriages and deaths (the Statutory Registers) are an essential resource for family historians and provide researchers with much valuable information which is not to be found in the English equivalents. Unfortunately, registration didn't start in Scotland until 1 January 1855 but this is more than made up for by the extra details that were recorded.

In addition to the information shown on English and Welsh birth certificates, Scottish certificates record:

- the time of birth
- the date and place of the parents' marriage

In the early years of civil registration in Scotland even more information was requested, but this level of detail turned out to be unsustainable. In 1855, the following additional details were recorded:

· the father's age and birthplace
· his previous issue, living and deceased (numbers and gender only)
· the mother's age and birthplace

This was quickly abandoned and these three questions, along with the date and place of the parents' marriage, were absent from birth certificates between 1856 and 1860. In 1861 this last item was reinstated.

It's not hard to see how useful this extra information is, as it provides a direct link between birth and marriage certificates which is wholly absent in England and Wales.

Scottish marriage certificates record one further, extremely useful piece of information: namely, the names and maiden surnames of the mothers of the bride and groom. They also include a specific question asking whether the parents of the bride and the groom are deceased, and, as with the birth records, there were some extra items in the early years that were soon abandoned:

· if a widower or a widow, whether second or third marriage (1855 only)
· children by each former marriage (numbers living and dead) (1855 only)
· the relationship of the couple getting married (if related) (1855 to 1860)

Since 1972, Scottish marriage certificates have recorded the bride and groom's dates of birth rather than their ages.

Unlike their English and Welsh counterparts, Scottish death certificates are simply packed with useful information, including:

· the marital status of the deceased
· their father's name, occupation and whether he is deceased

· their mother's name (including maiden surname) and whether she is deceased
· their spouse's name (including maiden surname where relevant)

Again, the early years of death registration saw an abundance of extra questions:

· the deceased's place of birth (1855 only)
· how long they had lived in the district in which they died (1855 only)
· the names and ages of their children or the age and year of death if the child pre-deceased their parent (1855 only)
· their burial place (1855 to 1860)

Unfortunately, the registrars soon found that all this was too much to manage and that in many cases the informants were unable to provide the required information with any degree of accuracy. And this is also a matter to consider with later Scottish death certificates – when a young man registers his grandfather's death, how likely is he to have known his grandfather's mother's maiden surname?

But despite this, it's pretty clear that all of this extra information on Scottish certificates is a real boon to those of us with ancestors from north of the border, making the difficult task of identifying individuals in the records, and building bridges from generation to generation, that much easier.

Scottish censuses are essentially no different, in terms of content, to the returns for England and Wales. The dates of the censuses are the same, the layout of the forms is almost identical and the same basic questions were asked.

Scottish parish registers, on the other hand, tend not to have been so well kept as their English counterparts. The earliest surviving registers date from 1538 but in the more remote areas, particularly in the Highlands and Islands, many of the registers don't start until the early 1800s.

Having said that, you do stand a good chance of finding a complete run of baptismal and marriage registers for your ancestors' parish from the mid 1600s onwards; burial registers, however, tend to be few and far between. Baptismal registers normally record the date of birth, and where burial registers survive they usually show the date of death. Parish registers almost always record women's maiden names, so that a typical entry in a baptismal register might start: 'Isabel, lawful daughter of Thomas Hunter and Catherine Miller...' The word 'lawful' indicates that Thomas and Catherine were married and that the birth was therefore legitimate. The word 'natural' was often used to indicate an illegitimate birth but sometimes you may have to look closer – the very absence of the word 'lawful' may be the only clue you get. Scottish parish registers are commonly referred to as Old Parish Registers (OPRs).

Wills and testaments in Scotland work in a slightly different way to those in England and Wales. A testament is the legal document that allows an executor to administer the deceased's estate. There are two types of testament: a testament testamentar is issued by the courts when the deceased left a will naming an executor; when the deceased died intestate (i.e. without leaving a will), an executor is appointed by the court and issued with a testament dative. Records survive from the early 1500s but it's fair to say that, over the years, only a small proportion of Scots have left wills.

There can be no doubt that, as a family historian, it pays to be Scottish. We've already looked at some of the extra details recorded on the major sources, but another huge advantage of using Scottish records is that women tended to keep their maiden surnames for most legal purposes; so not only in parish registers, but also in wills and testaments, and on gravestones, you should expect to see women's maiden names used as a matter of course – you may even come across this practice on some of the earlier census returns. As you can imagine, this makes identification of a particular couple in the records relatively straightforward.

There are two other great benefits of having Scottish ancestors: first of all, the vast majority of the key sources for Scottish family history are held in one building: the ScotlandsPeople Centre in Edinburgh. The Centre is run by the National Records of Scotland, an organisation formed in April 2011 by the amalgamation of The National Archives of Scotland (NAS) and General Register Office for Scotland (GROS).

Secondly, and even more important for those unfortunate enough not to be able to travel to Edinburgh, the same key sources are all available online, fully indexed and linked to digital images of the original documents. And better still, they can all be accessed on one site – ScotlandsPeople: www.scotlandspeople.gov.uk.

The site provides access to the following:

· births 1855–2009 (images to 1911)
· marriages1855–2009 (images to 1936)
· deaths 1855–2009 (images to 1961)
· baptisms (OPRs) 1538–1854
· marriages (OPRs) 1538–1854
· burials (OPRs) 1538–1854
· census returns 1841–1911
· wills and testaments 1513–1925

Also included are large numbers of Roman Catholic parish registers, records of Coats of Arms, the Valuation Rolls of 1915 and a large collection of 'Minor' records including 'overseas' births, marriages and deaths of Scottish citizens (including war deaths) dating from 1855.

The National Archives of Scotland (now part of the National Records of Scotland) holds a vast range of sources relating to land ownership, the Poor Law, nonconformist congregations, emigration and taxation, as well as over 500 years' worth of records from the Court of Sessions and other legal bodies.

Although the most important sources are centralised in Edinburgh, there is a wealth of useful material available in local record offices and libraries the length and breadth of Scotland, such as Glasgow's Mitchell Library and the city archives of Dundee and Aberdeen, to name but a few. Indeed, as in England and Wales, practically every major town in Scotland has a local studies centre that would be well worth visiting if your ancestors have come from that area.

Ireland
The situation in Ireland is somewhat less favourable for family historians, partly because so much of the basic source material has not survived, and partly because comparatively little of what does survive is available online.

Irish family history has suffered two great losses: one caused by a fire in Dublin during the Troubles in 1922 and the other the result of wholesale destruction by the Irish government.

A full census return of the whole of Ireland had been taken every 10 years since 1821, and from 1861 a question was included about religious denomination. It's possible that the sensitive nature of this question may have led to the unfortunate decision to destroy the returns for 1861, 1871, 1881 and 1891. Whatever the reason, the absence of this major source has left a gaping hole for Irish researchers. But worse was to come.

By 1922, the earlier census returns had been deposited with the Public Record Office (the forerunner of The National Archives of Ireland) and when a fire broke out that year at the Four Courts building in Dublin, they were tragically lost, along with countless other irreplaceable documents. The implications for Irish family history are enormous. Not only are there almost no surviving Victorian censuses (a few small fragments survive), but it has been estimated that around half of the Church of Ireland's parish registers also perished in the fire. When you add to this the loss of almost all Irish probate records from before 1858, as well as a huge collection of legal documents and medieval statute rolls, you begin to get an idea of how catastrophic the fire was for the study of Irish history in general.

But it's not all bad news. The civil registration records, which start in 1864, were held by the General Register Office for Ireland and were therefore unaffected by the fire. The 1901 and 1911 censuses (which were also held by the GRO at the time) have survived in full and are now held by The National Archives in Dublin. The returns have been fully indexed and digitised and are available to search, free of charge, at www.census.nationalarchives.ie.

The National Library of Ireland holds a large collection of Roman Catholic parish registers, and the surviving records of the Church of Ireland. The registers of the various nonconformist congregations, such as the Presbyterians, Methodists and Baptists are also extremely valuable sources. However, there is no single repository for these registers and tracking down any surviving records for a particular parish may involve visits to a number of different record offices.

A number of 'census substitutes' are available and go some way towards making up for the almost complete lack of the Victorian censuses. The most important of these is Griffith's Valuation, an extensive listing of the names of the occupiers and owners of land throughout Ireland from 1845 onwards. The Tithe Applotment Books predate these records by some 20 years and fulfil a similar purpose, although they cover a far smaller percentage of the population.

Irish civil registration records are practically identical in terms of layout and content to those of England and Wales. And although the full registration service started in 1864 (much later than elsewhere in the UK), it's worth noting that registration of non-Roman Catholic marriages began nearly 20 years earlier in 1845 – this is a significant source which should not be overlooked. Copies of birth, marriage and death certificates are available from the General Register Office for Ireland (www.groireland.ie).

Roots Ireland, the website of the Irish Family History Foundation (www.rootsireland.ie) provides access to over 19 million Irish records, including a large number of baptism, marriage and burial registers (both Roman Catholic and Church of Ireland), and the whole of Griffith's Valuation and the Tithe Applotment Books.

Irish Origins (www.irishorigins.com) also has a significant collection of Irish material, as do FindMyPast and Ancestory. The latter includes indexes to Irish civil registration records from 1864 (1845 for non-Catholic marriages) up to 1958.

As with other parts of the British Isles, Ireland has a vast range of useful local sources and is particularly fortunate to have the resources of a network of local heritage centres where you can get expert advice and guidance on researching your Irish ancestors.

Records relating to Northern Ireland are held separately for 1922 onwards. The Public Record Office of Northern Ireland (PRONI) has copies of a number of church registers, while civil registration records for Northern Ireland are held by the General Register Office (Northern Ireland).

The Channel Islands and the Isle of Man

Although they are included in the British Isles, Jersey, Guernsey (including Alderney and Sark) and the Isle of Man have never been part of the United Kingdom. Instead, they are classed as British Crown Dependencies.

Each of the islands has its own register offices, archives and libraries, with records of births, marriages and deaths, parish registers and wills, as well as significant collections of legal documents and records of local taxation and land ownership.

The census returns are held by The National Archives alongside the records for England and Wales and are therefore fully searchable on the major commercial websites. Microfilm copies of the censuses are held in the relevant local archives.

The GENUKI website (www.genuki.org.uk) is an excellent source of information about the vast range of material that is available for both the Channel Islands and the Isle of Man.

Share it

Since the 1970s when public interest in family history began to grow, many thousands of people have researched their ancestry. Sadly, the result of much of this research is now lying in boxes in attics or sitting on redundant hard drives.

All those notebooks and roughly drawn family trees, the certificates and census returns, copies of wills and clippings from newspapers – all lovingly and painstakingly researched and now gathering dust. And the life's work that your late uncle meticulously entered onto his computer 10 years ago, unwittingly wiped when the PC was sold after his death.

But it doesn't have to be like this: nowadays, publishing the results of your research is easier than ever before. You don't need to have access to expensive, hi-tech equipment and you don't have to negotiate a deal with a publisher. All you need is access to a computer, a touch of imagination and a fair amount of time on your hands.

The first step is to get hold of a good family tree software package (there are several on the market, and they're all very similar). You can use it to create family trees and to organise your data in a way that makes it easy to access. Apart from anything else, this will help you to plan your online research and make the most of your trips to record offices and libraries. But perhaps the most useful aspect of your software package is that it will save your data as a 'gedcom' (GEnealogical Data COMmunication) file. This format was developed by the Church of Jesus Christ of Latter-day Saints in the 1980s and has become the 'industry standard' for handling family history data files.

Once you have a gedcom file for your family tree, sharing your research with others becomes a relatively straightforward matter, and there are a number of different ways you can do it. You can send copies of the file to relatives or other interested researchers, who, providing they have some suitable software themselves, will be able to open it on their own device. Another approach is to use one of the many websites that allow you to upload your gedcom file for the whole world to see. Before you do this, you need to find out how your data will be displayed and what control you will have over it (can you make changes or even remove names?) and you might want to check that your data won't be used to someone else's commercial advantage.

The more adventurous among you might even consider creating your own websites; and don't ignore the enduring power of the printed word – there are several companies that offer affordable solutions to publishing your research. Small print-runs of illustrated booklets can be a cheap and effective way of sharing your family's story with friends, relatives and other researchers.

The other side of the coin to all of this is that you can access the results of other people's research in any of the formats mentioned above. You may find that there are distant cousins out there who are researching the same people, and – you never know – they might have found their way around the brick wall that's been holding you up for months.

Finally, if there's no one in your family to carry on your research you might consider making a specific bequest in your will about what to do with your research once you've gone. The Society of Genealogists actively encourages people to arrange for their research (organised or not!) to be deposited in their library in London. So, act now and don't let your family history end up in a box, hidden away – or worse still, on a bonfire!

Passenger list from the SS Carmania on her voyage from Liverpool to New York in 1922 showing Charles Darwin's grandson, Bernard Darwin, the Golf Correspondent for The Times.

Chapter 13

Moving there and moving here: Emigrants and immigrants

Births, marriages and deaths at sea and overseas
Emigration
Immigration
Criminal 'emigrants'

It's tempting to picture our ancestors living out their lives in the English countryside, working on the land, going to church on Sundays, perhaps finding time for the occasional drink at the local inn. Or we might imagine the later generations who were forced off the land and moved into the bustling Victorian towns and cities where life was perhaps less pleasant for them, with no escape from cradle to grave.

And this is fine if your ancestors happened to spend the whole of their lives in these lands, without setting foot on foreign soil. But of course, the population has never been that settled, and it's highly likely that even among your English or Welsh relatives, some of them will have migrated during the course of their lives – within the British Isles, across the Channel to the European continent, over the Atlantic Ocean or even further afield to India and the Far East.

And the other side of the coin is that some of your own ancestors may have moved from another country in order to settle in the British Isles.

In this chapter we'll take a look at the millions of people who left these shores to start new lives in Australia, South Africa, New Zealand, the Americas and elsewhere. We'll also look at those immigrants who have arrived over the centuries: from countries such as France, Italy, Germany, Poland and Russia, and, more recently, from the Indian sub-continent, Africa and the Caribbean.

Much of this movement has been of people seeking refuge from political or religious persecution, but perhaps just as many of the individuals have been tradesmen, artisans, craftsmen or other kinds of economic migrants in search of opportunities to earn a decent living.

We also need to consider what we might call 'temporary migrants' – people who travelled overseas, spent some time away and then returned. They may have been working or simply travelling abroad, or perhaps they were 'serious' emigrants who decided after a few years that life in the new country wasn't for them and set out on the long voyage back home – this happened more often than you might expect.

Finally, we'll take a look at a special class of migrants – the thousands of men and women who were transported beyond the seas as a punishment for their crimes.

Births, marriages and deaths at sea and overseas

As well as attempting to perform the unenviable task of recording every birth, marriage and death that takes place in England and Wales, the General Register Office has responsibility for registering events relating to English and Welsh citizens that take place overseas and at sea.

The records created by this ongoing process form a vast and diverse collection of registers, which includes:

· births, marriages and deaths registered by the British Forces and the British Consul or High Commission in the country where they took place, from 1849;

· deaths that occurred in the Boer War and both World Wars;

· British Army regimental records of births, baptisms and marriages dating back to 1761;

· marine births and deaths, from 1837, which took place on British-registered vessels;

· aircraft births and deaths, from 1948, which took place on British-registered aircraft.

These registers are by no means a comprehensive record of all such events and they do not, as a rule, include records of births, marriages and deaths which took place in Commonwealth countries such as Australia, Canada, New Zealand, South Africa or the Indian sub-continent. Nor do they record events relating to permanent emigrants, so the marriage or death of your ancestor's brother who emigrated to Argentina in the 1870s is unlikely to be found here. In each of these cases, events involving British citizens would have been registered locally and the British authorities would have considered them perfectly valid for all legal purposes.

Nevertheless, the 'overseas' registers do contain many thousands of records of English and Welsh citizens whose births, marriages and deaths were registered at a British embassy or on board a British vessel, and they also contain records of servicemen and women and their families who were stationed overseas.

The registers also include records of war deaths, with the registers of British soldiers who died in the First World War representing a significant proportion of them. The certificates themselves contain very little information of real interest to family historians and often give the soldier's place of death as simply 'France' or 'Flanders', but they do show the age and date of death, along with the man's name, rank and number, so they can be a useful starting point for further research into an ancestor's military service records.

Each of these sources is indexed separately and it wasn't until 1966 that the GRO started to compile single annual indexes to all registered overseas events. The good news is that the indexes are all available on the FindMyPast website and can also be seen on microfiche in a number of record offices and libraries around the country.

The National Archives also holds a large amount of overseas material which family historians would find extremely useful if only they knew of its existence. Known as the 'Miscellaneous Overseas Registers', this assorted collection of registers (in record series RG 32–RG 36) was originally transferred from the General Register Office in the 1970s. These are largely non-statutory records of births (and baptisms), marriages, deaths (and burials) of British subjects which took place overseas and at sea. The collection includes a number of registers from former British protectorates in Africa and Asia, and the oldest volume in the series is a register from The Hague which was started in 1627. More records are added periodically, and the most recent dates from 1969.

The GRO's marine registers are complemented by another source held by The National Archives at Kew: the records of births, marriages and deaths of passengers at sea from 1845 to 1890 in record series BT 158–BT 160. These are mainly duplicates of the GRO's registers but are well worth searching for additional entries which may not have been forwarded to the relevant General Register Office. The registers of deaths at sea together with the miscellaneous overseas registers are fully indexed and available online as part of the BMDregisters website.

Another large collection of overseas registers of baptisms, marriages and burials, known as the International Memoranda and formerly in the possession of the Bishop of London, is now held by the London Metropolitan Archives.

The British Library in London is home to a remarkable collection of material compiled by the British authorities in India between 1600 and 1947. Registers of the baptisms, marriages and burials of Anglo-Indians in the various Presidencies of Bengal (from 1713), Madras (from 1698) and Bombay (from 1709) are among the archives that were transferred to the British Library following Indian independence in 1947, along with volumes of wills, records of the Indian Army and Navy and civil service appointment books. If your ancestor was one of the thousands of British men and women included in these records, you're likely to discover some surprising details about their lives in the Raj.

All of these sources are worth investigating and you can find out more about them in *Tracing Your Ancestors in The National Archives* by Amanda Bevan and *The British Overseas* published by Guildhall Library.

Emigration

As we have seen, Scotland and Ireland have always had their own legal systems (which led to the creation of their own distinct records). However, the Acts of Union of 1707 (with Scotland) and 1800 (with Ireland) saw the various parts of the British Isles joining together to form a single state. And this meant that movement from Glasgow to Belfast, from Cork to Bristol or from Manchester to Edinburgh did not constitute emigration (or immigration, for that matter) any more than moving from Durham to Liverpool did – it was simply a case of migrating from one place to another within the same nation-state. So don't expect to find any records of your Irish 'immigrant' ancestor's arrival in England – he wasn't an immigrant and his journey from Roscommon wouldn't have resulted in the creation of any sort of documentation.

Tracing records of people who moved further afield is, unfortunately, rarely an easy task. Your best chance of finding any surviving documentation of their movement is amongst the records of the country of arrival. The British government was not terribly concerned about people leaving these shores, whereas the authorities in Australia, for example, kept very good records. However, The National Archives in Kew does hold a wide variety of records relating to emigration:

· passenger lists for ships leaving the UK (1890 to 1960)
· registers of convicts transported to Australia (1787 to 1868)
· Colonial Office records of correspondence (1817 to 1896)
· Poor Law Union papers concerning assisted emigration schemes (1834–90)
· Foreign Office passport registers (1795 to 1898)

Other sources include Plantation Books, Privy Council Registers, Colonial State Papers and the records of various child migration schemes (mainly to Canada) between 1869 and 1930. These records contain thousands of files and registers, including references to thousands, possibly even millions of people who left the UK to settle in other countries around the world. The problem with using this material is that hardly any of it is indexed and your chances of finding anything about a particular individual are somewhat remote.

In recent years, however, various websites have made a number of important databases available, making the whole process of tracing emigrants and immigrants from their place of origin to their new place of settlement easier than it has ever been.

FindMyPast has indexed and digitised The National Archives' collection of Outwards Passenger Lists (record series BT 27), which covers ships leaving British ports (including Irish ports until 1921) on inter-continental voyages from 1890 to 1960. Some of the earlier lists are somewhat lacking in detail, but the amount of information recorded about each passenger increased over the years and, as people tended to travel in family groups, the lists can be extremely useful.

Ancestry has a remarkable collection of material relating to emigration from the British Isles (and many other places in Europe), mainly compiled from records held in the destination countries. There are literally hundreds of databases available recording the arrival of passengers in ports up and down both coasts of America, as well as various destinations in Canada and Australia – all fully searchable by name.

The Society of Genealogists has what is possibly the UK's best collection of material relating to British emigrants. Much of this is printed material, published in the countries where the emigrants ended up. Probably the most important of these are the volumes of ships' passenger lists, recording the names (and sometimes the ages and places of origin) of emigrants to the US and Canada from the 1500s. These lists are by no means comprehensive, but they do contain many thousands of names and there's a good chance of finding a distant relative listed here.

Immigration

In the past few years a huge amount of effort has gone into making the records of people settling in the British Isles more accessible. The results can be found on a website called Moving Here (www.movinghere.org.uk).

The site provides access to original documents relating to immigration and also includes photographs and personal stories. Moving Here concentrates on the Caribbean, Irish, Jewish and South Asian communities in Britain over the past 200 years, but there are plans to cover other immigrant groups in the future. It's important to remember that once an immigrant arrived in this country, they would be treated in the same way as anyone else as far as civil registration, census returns and probate records are concerned.

For many of us, the first clue that we have an immigrant ancestor may come from an unexpected birthplace on a census return. The census enumerators' instructions were to give just the country of birth, but if you're lucky you might get the name of a particular town or village, which will give you an excellent lead for further research in the native country.

Many immigrants soon adopted 'anglicised' versions of their names; this is a particular problem with Jewish immigrants arriving from Eastern Europe in the latter half of the 19th century and it can provide you with almost insurmountable difficulties. In English law, people are free to call themselves by any name they choose, providing they're not doing so for fraudulent purposes. Very few people who changed their names did so officially, by deed poll, and of those who did, only a small percentage chose to have the record of their change of name 'enrolled'. So it's best not to hold out too much hope of finding anything here.

As with the records of emigration that we looked at above, the best sources for information about your immigrant ancestors are held by The National Archives. The most important records are:

- records of denizations and naturalisations (1500s to 1980)
- passenger lists for ships arriving in the UK (1878 to 1960)
- certificates of aliens (1836 to 1852)
- entry books (1794 to 1909)
- changes of name by deed poll (1851 to 2003)

Several early series of records among the State Papers and Chancery Rolls also include references to immigrant communities in Britain.

You should be warned that these documents may promise more than they actually deliver, as the fact is that the records held by The National Archives record only a very small percentage of people arriving in this country over the years. But if you do find a mention of your ancestors, particularly in the post-1844 naturalisation case files (HO 1, HO 45, HO 144 and HO 405), you could be in for yet another of those genealogical treats. The Home Office made very thorough enquiries into the background of everyone applying to become a British citizen and the results of their investigations have been preserved in these files. Details such as age, place of birth, parentage and a physical description are usually given, together with information about how long the person has been in the UK and the various addresses they've lived at since their arrival. You should also expect to find testimonials from people who knew your ancestors and were willing to declare that they were suitable candidates for British citizenship. And the good news is that these files, together with the Duplicate Certificates of Naturalisation covering the years 1870–1980 (HO 334 and HO 449) are now fully indexed and accessible via The National Archives' online catalogue, making searching for your immigrant ancestors easier than ever.

The bad news is that the vast majority of people arriving in the UK did not undergo the naturalisation process. Nevertheless, since a search is now so easy to do, there's really no excuse for not doing some exploring.

The Inwards Passenger Lists held by The National Archives in record series BT 26 are fully searchable on the Ancestry website, with links to digital images of the lists themselves. Ancestry has also digitised the Certificates of Aliens and other 'returns and papers' covering the years 1836–1869 (HO 2 and HO 3) which are fully indexed, and the Aliens' entry books for 1794–1921 (HO 5 and HO 25–28) which can be browsed as digital microfilm. These are far from being comprehensive records of immigrants to the UK, but they are a good starting point for a search.

If you're fortunate enough to have Huguenot ancestry, you'll find that an enormous amount of material has been published by the Huguenot Society of Great Britain and Ireland. As well as the registers of the various Huguenot communities in England and Ireland, the Society has published volumes of indexes to Letters of Denization and Acts of Naturalisation, Lists of Aliens Resident in London and Returns of Strangers in the Metropolis, all of which also include references to non-Huguenots.

The subject of naturalisation and immigration is highly complex and there simply isn't the space to go into any real detail in a book of this size. For a more in-depth coverage, see Roger Kershaw and Mark Pearsall's excellent guide, *Immigrants and Aliens: A Guide to Sources on UK Immigration and Citizenship*, which is published by The National Archives.

Criminal 'emigrants'

The idea of transporting criminals 'beyond the seas' as an alternative to the death penalty started as early as 1614, when the British authorities began to ship convicts to the plantations in America and the West Indies. Transportation to America continued until 1775 and it has been estimated that as many as 50,000 men (and a smaller number of women) suffered this punishment over the years.

Peter Wilson Coldham has published two books which together provide a comprehensive index to the surviving records: *The Complete Book of Emigrants in Bondage 1614–1775* and *Bonded Passengers to America*. The books were compiled from sources held by The National Archives (assize records, patent rolls and treasury books and papers) and the London Metropolitan Archives (transportation bonds and landing certificates). Copies of the books are likely to be found in larger record offices.

13 May 1787 is perhaps not a date that many people in the UK would recognise, but it's arguably one of the most important dates in British history. It's the day on which the 'First Fleet' set sail for Australia: 11 ships, with a total of 1044 people on board – 696 of them convicted prisoners bound for the new penal colony of New South Wales.

This was just the first of many convict transportations to Australia – 165,000 men and women are known to have been shipped to the various Australian penal colonies during the 80 years between 1788 and 1868.

The records of these transportations, along with the associated trial records, the records of the notorious prison hulks on which many of the convicts were imprisoned prior to transportation and the records of the newly established colonies themselves have left us with a remarkably detailed picture of the history of transportation to Australia.

Ancestry has indexed and digitised the most important of these records, including the Convict Transportation Registers (in record series HO 11), the New South Wales and Tasmania Convict Musters (HO 10) and the 1828 and 1841 New South Wales census returns (copies held by the State Records Authority of New South Wales).

Details of the original trial can usually be tracked down by searching the Home Office's Criminal Trial Registers, which are held by The National Archives in record series HO 26 and HO 27. These records cover the years 1791–1892 and are fully searchable on the Ancestry website. They provide the name of the accused, the nature of the alleged crime and the verdict and sentence, as well as details of the court in which they were tried and the date of the trial. This information can be used to identify the relevant Assize court records, which are also held by The National Archives.

DID YOU KNOW?

Significant immigration from the Caribbean began when colonial service personnel stayed on in Britain after the Second World War. Immigration was encouraged from 1948 onwards, to solve post-war labour shortages and alleviate unemployment in the West Indies. When the labour market reached a surplus, the 1962 Commonwealth Immigrants Act began the process of restricting entry.

Hitting the wall

Whether you've been researching your family history for 10 years or 10 weeks you are almost certain to have experienced that dreadful moment when a search you're fully expecting to bear fruit turns up absolutely nothing.

In the old days, you might have been searching the GRO's birth, marriage and death indexes, or winding through reels of microfilm looking for an ancestor in the census. You turn the page, fully expecting to find what you're looking for – and there it isn't!

Now, in the digital age, it's more likely that you'll end up with the dreaded 'no results' screen on your computer but either way, you've been stopped in your stride – it feels like you've just stepped on a stair that isn't there.

You might try a few other ideas and quickly come up with the answer – but what if you don't? What if nothing that you try works out? What if, months, or even years later, you still don't have the answer? What if the person you're looking for seems to have appeared from thin air; seems to have arrived on this planet as a fully formed adult with no past?

Welcome to the world of the family history brick wall.

There's rarely an easy answer, but there are a number of techniques that you would be well advised to familiarise yourself with. We've already looked at the 'less is more' principle for searching online databases (see page 120) and perhaps the best example of this is a search where you leave an important field, such as the surname, blank. This will return a list of results where all the other details (forename, age and place of birth, for example) match your search, leaving you a list in which can hopefully identify a mistranscribed surname or spot a clue that you can follow up elsewhere.

Another approach might be to search by surname only and hope to pick up a spelling of the first name that you weren't expecting, or perhaps find that your target is listed by his initials only.

Family historians need to learn to tackle brick walls in the same manner as a mathematician or a scientist. You need to build up a theory and then attempt to knock it down. The important thing to remember is that it is just a theory. Don't make the mistake of leaping to conclusions without firm evidence.

Quite often, the difficult part is coming up with a suitable theory in the first place. How do you go about identifying a possible candidate to be your missing ancestor? This is where a technique called 'family reconstruction' comes in. The idea is to extract every possible reference to a surname in a particular area from every conceivable source: parish registers, wills, manorial documents, poor law records, taxation records, deeds – all the usual suspects. Then you attempt to put them into distinct family groups and start to build up theories about relationships between them. The idea is that, eventually, you can identify the most likely group for your ancestor to belong to and take it from there.

The crucial thing to remember is that you should always try to disprove a theory rather than try to prove it. As Sherlock Holmes put it:

It is an old maxim of mine that when you have excluded the impossible, whatever remains, however improbable, must be the truth.

Family reconstruction might be seen as a 'focused' approach to tackling a problem but there's also what we might call the 'scattergun' strategy. A Google search is the perfect example of this: you simply enter the surname together with the place of interest, click search and see what it throws up. It may not be the most scientific approach, but sometimes it works. And that, surely, is all that matters.

Search for *Type:* Births *Surname:* darwin *First name(s):* george

Whilst FreeBMD makes every effort to ensure accurate transcription, errors exist in both the original index and the transcription. You are advised to verify the reference given from a copy of the index before ordering a certificate. If an entry has the symbol ᴳ next to it you can view the scan of the GRO index page from which the transcription was made in order to verify the reference. Click on the ᴳ symbol to view the scan.

If you are SURE that our transcription(s) below differs from the GRO index, you can submit a correction request by clicking on the Info button to the right of the entry in question.

Surname	First name(s)	District	Vol	Page		
Births Jun 1840 (>99%)						
Darwin	George Heary	Huddersfield	22	303	Info	ᴳ
Births Sep 1844 (>99%)						
Darwin	George	Sheffield	22	567	Info	ᴳ
Births Sep 1845 (>99%)						
Darwin	George Howard	Bromley	5	49	Info	ᴳ
Births Sep 1847 (>99%)						

Results from a search for the birth of George Darwin on the FreeBMD website

Chapter 14

The whole world is out there: Family history and the Internet

Researching in cyberspace
Search engines
Portals
The individual and the Web
Mailing lists and message boards
This ever-changing world

Throughout this book you will have come across countless references to family history websites. Collectively, these websites provide access to most of the key sources for UK family history research. Ancestry and FindMyPast are the market leaders, each boasting millions of online records, but there are other commercial sites such as The Genealogist, British Origins, Genes Reunited and, of course, ScotlandsPeople and Roots Ireland (a not-for-profit site) with their specialist coverage of Scotland and Ireland respectively. And then there are the free sites, with FamilySearch leading the way, and volunteer-driven projects such as FreeBMD and UKBMD. Censuses, births, marriages and deaths, wills, parish registers, passenger lists, directories, military service records – the list is endless, and all of them are available 24 hours a day, 7 days a week, 52 weeks a year from the comfort of your own home.

The major sites have such vast and diverse collections of databases that to list them here would be a futile exercise. New records are being added all the time so any list would be out of date within a matter of weeks. In truth, the best guide to what's available on the Internet is the Internet itself!

So the aim of this chapter is to give you some tips on the best way to approach the Internet and to look at some dos and don'ts.

Researching online

It has been said that family history is the Internet's second most popular pursuit – no prizes for guessing what the most popular is – and it is hardly surprising that family history holds this position. It's almost as if the Internet was designed with family historians in mind. It enables people to share information, to ask questions and get quick answers, to interrogate vast databases and pull out the important information, to view the actual images of documents written hundreds of years ago – all of this (and much more) makes the Internet a truly indispensable tool.

And the amount of information out there is growing every day. Hardly a week passes without the launch of a new website offering access to yet another important source. But perhaps the biggest advance in recent years has been the development of databases which provide access to scanned digital images of original historical documents.

Family history websites can be divided into five basic types:

· sites with access to databases linked to digital images of primary source material, via an index;
· sites consisting of indexes to primary sources, sometimes with full transcripts;
· sites providing advice and guidance on using records;
· sites giving access to the results of an individual's personal research;
· sites providing links to other sites.

Viewing a scanned image of an original document is, in many ways, as good as looking at the real thing. You can view the document at your leisure and take your time to think about what it's telling you – and you're not relying on someone else's interpretation.

But some sites restrict you from browsing backwards and forwards through successive pages of the document – the digital equivalent of flicking through the pages – and this can make it difficult to understand how your page fits into the original context. A good researcher would always want to have a look at the census pages before and after the one that includes their ancestors, just to get a feeling for the type of area where they were living.

Although some of the websites that provide access to transcripts of original documents are undoubtedly a major asset to family history research, the details they give you are no substitute for viewing the document itself. And if the person who transcribed and indexed the document couldn't read a particular name, or if they made an error in the transcription, you might have real problems finding what you were looking for in the first place. Always check the original sources, think about where the information has come from and, most important of all, question everything.

So how do you find all the information that's out there? There are a number of different ways, each of which has its advantages. The main two are:

· search engines, such as Google
· 'portal' or 'directory' sites such as GENUKI or Cyndi's List

Search engines

These are the Internet's gift to family historians. They allow us to find information about our ancestors in a way that was simply unimaginable just a few years ago. The effortless act of entering your name into a search engine can provide you with links to hundreds of websites containing references to that name. Of course, the success of this basic approach depends on how common your name is – you wouldn't expect to get any meaningful results with names such as Williams or Jones. And if the surname is also a place name, a descriptive name or an occupation, like Hampshire, Brown or Baker, then you're going to have to think about adding some extra search terms: a first name, a place or even the words 'family history'. This technique can produce effective results, but you certainly shouldn't rely on it or think of it as a foolproof method of searching the Internet.

In order to use a search engine effectively for your family history research, you need to understand a little bit about how search engines gather their information. A search engine like Google uses a special type of robot programme called a spider or 'knowledge-bot' to 'crawl' through the World Wide Web following links and retrieving as much information as it can from the pages it visits. When you enter your search terms, Google checks its vast database and presents you with a list of 'hits'. What the spider can't do is type or think for itself, so when it encounters a search screen, it is unable to interrogate it in the way that you or I would.

Another important concept is known as the 'invisible web'. When we carry out a search in an online database, the results we see are created on what is known as a dynamic page. It didn't exist before we ran the search and it will disappear when we move away from it. Google can only index 'stable' URLs, so the data produced by the search is effectively 'invisible' to its spiders. FamilySearch is a good example of this. You may be able to find your great-great-grandfather's baptism, but if you put his name into Google, you wouldn't find the relevant entry in the list of results.

So you can't use search engines to search the contents of an online database, but you can use a search engine to find the relevant databases. Try typing in the subject and place that you're interested in and see what you get.

Portals

An alternative approach to finding information on the Internet is to use a portal site. The two most important for family historians are GENUKI (www.genuki.org.uk) and Cyndi's List (www.cyndislist.com).

GENUKI (which stands for Genealogy UK and Ireland) is a vital resource for anyone with UK ancestry. The site is organised geographically. Each county has its own section, with pages covering topics such as archives and libraries, church records, civil registration and maps. Although GENUKI does have much useful material of its own to offer the family historian, the main purpose of the site is to serve as a portal to other sites. The site is entirely run by volunteers and therefore its coverage is better for some counties than for others, but wherever your family came from, you're almost certain to find links to sources that you didn't even know existed.

Cyndi's List is an American site which works like a directory, each entry taking the form of a link to another website. Every conceivable family history topic has its own section and the range of subjects covered is quite simply astonishing. The site currently has links to more than 300,000 sites, and although much of this is dedicated to American research, there's still some excellent coverage of UK sources.

The individual and the Web

The Internet is also home to thousands of personal websites, and this aspect of the Internet is both one of its strengths and one of its weaknesses.

Most of these sites are made up of information that has been well researched and, in some cases, well documented – if you're lucky you may come across one that relates to your own ancestors. If you do, it could open up new avenues of research and possibly even put you in contact with some distant cousins in California. Unfortunately there are also thousands of websites containing research which is at best guesswork and at worst pure fabrication. There's a danger that once this sort of inaccurate information about an individual or a family is published on the Internet it assumes an authority and authenticity which is undeserved and is liable to be regurgitated on countless other sites. So, as with any other resources that you use in the course of your research, you should always check the source of the information – if there doesn't seem to be one, treat it with extreme caution!

Mailing lists and message boards

Thanks to the Internet it is now easier than ever to get in touch with other people who are researching the same surnames, or even the same family, as you. Message boards and mailing lists enable us to contact fellow researchers from all corners of the world and to share information with them – all in a matter of minutes and at the click of a mouse. It really couldn't be any easier.

There's a subtle difference between mailing lists and message boards. A mailing list is an interactive forum which you can subscribe to (for free) and immediately post queries. Then you simply sit back and wait for the answers to your query from other 'listers' to drop into your inbox. If you feel that you have something to contribute yourself, you can post your own replies to other messages. Don't forget about the time differences around the world and don't expect instant replies. If you're going to get any responses they'll probably appear within the first few days, but some people only check their emails at weekends, so don't give up too soon.

Some lists are very busy. This is, of course, largely a good thing, but you may find that receiving 20 or 30 emails a day is just too much for you to cope with. Other lists have very little traffic and you may find that several days or weeks pass without a message being posted.

Most of the people who contribute to family history mailing lists are keen and enthusiastic researchers like you, but they may have been on the list for years and they may have developed an encyclopaedic knowledge of the most important local sources. And you never know who you'll find on a mailing list – some of the world's leading experts on family history are regular contributors to mailing lists.

There are a few basic rules and guidelines that you should be aware of before you post your first message on a mailing list:

- Don't use html (hyper-text markup language) or fancy colours and fonts – plain text is always best.
- Never attach files to your messages – these can be harmful to other listers' computers.
- Respect other people's views – you're quite free to disagree, but keep it civilised.
- Don't expect people to do research for you without offering something in exchange.
- Don't post off-topic messages – make sure that your messages are relevant to the list.
- Don't post messages advertising a commercial product – it may be OK to mention a new publication, as long as it's relevant, but be careful how you go about it!

Most mailing lists are monitored, and if inappropriate behaviour is detected the list owner will usually give the perpetrator a first warning. If they break the rules again they could find that their future posts are blocked.

All of this comes under the term 'netiquette', which essentially means that you should observe the same standards of behaviour in cyberspace as you would practise in 'real life'.

Message boards work in a similar way to mailing lists but they allow you to post a message on a website which anyone can then see – people don't have to subscribe to a list in order to be able to read and respond to it. You're less likely to get quick answers to your queries, but searching message boards is pretty straightforward and you're quite likely to find some useful contacts out there.

Once you start looking around, you'll find that the range of subjects covered by family history mailing lists and message boards is huge. There are lists that cover whole counties or individual towns; there are lists dedicated to thousands of individual surnames; there are boards devoted to such topics as adoptions, DNA research, shipwrecks and medieval history. If a topic has a family history slant to it, you'll probably find a mailing list or a message board dedicated to it.

And by far the best way to find out about the vast range of these lists and message boards is to visit the biggest and best selection on the Internet at www.rootsweb.com. Rootsweb, which is now hosted by Ancestry, boasts over 30,000 genealogy mailing lists and more than 160,000 message boards. And if there isn't a board for your own surname, you might want to consider starting one and becoming a board administrator. Rootsweb is also an excellent resource in its own right, with links to personal research pages and thousands of family trees that you can view online.

DID YOU KNOW?
Nowadays, a growing number of researchers are extending their investigations beyond their own ancestors to research everyone with a particular surname. This approach to family history research (known as a One-Name Study) can help you to understand where your surname originated and how it developed and spread around the country.

This ever-changing world

The pace of change when it comes to technology and the Internet is now so fast – even in the 'sleepy' world of family history – that any attempt to document it must remain – in a paradoxical phrase – permanently provisional. How this will impact on the future of online family history research is impossible to predict, but there are some good published guides to help you keep track of the latest electronic developments, notably *The Genealogist's Internet* by Peter Christian, published by The National Archives.

In the end

We've come to the end of this book, but in some ways the journey has only just begun. It's true that some people take up family history research only to drop it after a few months, but most of us are in it for the long haul. Once you catch the bug it's difficult to shake off – and I'm not sure that anyone has ever found a cure.

You sometimes hear people saying that they finished researching their family tree years ago, which sounds like an odd statement to me. After all, since family history is essentially a process of working backwards through the generations, unless someone has successfully traced their ancestry back either to Adam and Eve or to the first micro-organism to emerge from the primordial soup, I don't really see how they can possibly have finished.

And 'real' family historians never admit defeat. It's inevitable that from time to time in the course of your research you will come up against problems that you just can't solve, questions that you can't answer. But what you really mean is that you haven't found the answer to the problem yet. Don't give up: the answer is out there!

Researching your family history is supposed to be fun – I hope this book has convinced you of that, if nothing else. But I also hope that the need to take your research seriously has been brought home: the need to adhere to the principles of good research; to question the 'facts' that you unearth; to think logically about what you've discovered; and to understand how the vast range of historical documents that we've looked at can be used most effectively.

There's a danger that our family history research can become too important to us and that what begins as a harmless hobby can cross the line to become an obsession. We just need to make sure that it doesn't become an addiction. I haven't come across any branches of Family Historians Anonymous springing up around the country, but it may just be a matter of time! Seriously, you shouldn't let it take over your life – try not to turn your partner into a family history widow or widower and don't spend more time with your long-dead ancestors than you do with your living family.

But if you feel that you really need something to bridge the gap between the last visit to The National Archives and the next, there are plenty of things you can do. Hundreds of books have been written on various aspects of family history research and there are now half a dozen or so magazines on the market. You can join your local family history society, which will almost certainly hold regular meetings, offering advice clinics and lectures as well as the opportunity to meet fellow researchers and share experiences.

Take time to explore the Internet – you will be amazed by the amount of potentially useful material that's out there, just waiting to be discovered. Many people fear that the Internet is making family history research too easy, and it's certainly true that you can do a lot of the basic research much more quickly than ever before. But surely this is a good thing if it gives us more time to investigate the more interesting records, those less obvious sources which make our hobby so worthwhile.

Many people also believe that the growth of the Internet and the proliferation of online family history databases will be the death of archives. But there's certainly no sign of that happening so far, as visitor numbers at record offices around the country remain high. I think that there are a number of very good reasons for this. For a start, the documents that can be accessed online represent a mere drop in the ocean compared to the volume of material in record offices that hasn't even been microfilmed, let alone digitally scanned. Secondly, record offices are home to some of the greatest minds in the archival world – where would family historians be without the help, advice and guidance of this great army of experts?

Finally, and I think most importantly of all, family history should be a social pursuit. No trip to a record office is complete without a lunch hour spent discussing your latest finds with a total stranger – although, of course, no serious family historian would ever stop working for a whole hour! So make the best of both worlds: embrace the Internet and all it offers but don't forget the more traditional resources of the record offices. And whatever else you do, don't forget to enjoy your research and the pleasure of meeting like-minded people.

Glossary

Admon See LETTERS OF ADMINISTRATION.

Adoption The process of taking legal responsibility for another person's child.

Annuitant A person who receives a fixed sum of money at regular intervals.

Apportionments Documents produced to accompany TITHE MAPS, dating from around 1840 and listing owners and occupiers of land in each tithe district.

Apprentice A person who is learning a particular trade by working for someone else. See also JOURNEYMAN; MASTER.

Archdeaconry An administrative unit of the CHURCH OF ENGLAND.

Bachelor An unmarried man.

Banns The public declaration of the intent by two people to get married. The calling of banns in the parish church on three successive Sundays was introduced by the terms of HARDWICKE'S MARRIAGE ACT.

BIVRI British Isles Vital Records Index.

BL British Library.

Census An official count of the population. Carried out in the UK every 10 years since 1801 (except 1941).

Census returns The records created as part of the process of taking a CENSUS.

Certificates Official documents recording major life events i.e. births, marriages and deaths.

Church of England The established state church in England. Also referred to as the Anglican Church.

Church of Jesus Christ of Latter-day Saints The official name of the Mormon Church, founded in La Fayette, New York in 1850 by Joseph Smith. Important to family historians for their network of FAMILYSEARCH CENTRES and the huge database known as FAMILYSEARCH.

Civil registration The legal process of registering births, marriages and deaths, introduced in England and Wales in 1837.

Clandestine marriage A term commonly used to describe marriages conducted by disreputable clergyman which took place in areas outside the control of the CHURCH OF ENGLAND. They were outlawed by the passing of HARDWICKE'S MARRIAGE ACT. Also known as IRREGULAR MARRIAGES.

Condition A category used in census returns, indicating whether married, single, widowed or divorced.

County record office A major repository holding important records relating to the people and history of a particular county.

CRO COUNTY RECORD OFFICE.

Deanery An administrative unit of the CHURCH OF ENGLAND.

Death duty A series of taxes raised by the INLAND REVENUE on the estate of the deceased.

Denization The act of making someone a citizen of the country. Originally the same as NATURALISATION, but came to imply that citizenship had been granted by the Crown.

Diocese An administrative unit of the CHURCH OF ENGLAND.

Ecclesiastical Relating to the CHURCH OF ENGLAND.

Enumerator Official responsible for collecting and returning CENSUS information.

Family Bible A large Bible with pages for recording family events, notably births, marriages and deaths.

Family history centres A worldwide network of research centres provided by the CHURCH OF JESUS CHRIST OF LATTER-DAY SAINTS.

Family history society An organisation formed to provide advice and guidance to family historians in a specific area. Most societies produce lists and indexes of relevant local material and hold regular meetings.

FamilySearch A database containing records of births, baptisms, marriages, deaths and burials, compiled by the CHURCH OF JESUS CHRIST OF LATTER-DAY SAINTS.

FFHS Federation of Family History Societies. An umbrella organisation representing the interests of local FAMILY HISTORY SOCIETIES.

First Avenue House The home of the Principal Registry of the Family Division, providing access to records of wills proved in England and Wales since 1858.

Full age Aged 21 or over.

Genealogical Society of Utah The genealogical section of the CHURCH OF JESUS CHRIST OF LATTER-DAY SAINTS.

General Register Office Formed in 1837 to oversee the civil registration process. Also responsible for organising census returns since 1861.

GENUKI A major website for family historians. Stands for Geneaology in the UK and Ireland.

GRO GENERAL REGISTER OFFICE.

GRO indexes The indexes to births, marriages and deaths created by the GENERAL REGISTER OFFICE.

GSU GENEALOGICAL SOCIETY OF UTAH.

Hardwicke's Marriage Act An Act passed in 1753 which outlawed CLANDESTINE MARRIAGES in England and Wales.

HMC Historical Manuscripts Commission – now part of THE NATIONAL ARCHIVES.

Huguenots French Protestants who fled to England to escape religious persecution.

Illegitimate A term used to describe a person whose parents were not legally married at the time of his or her birth.

Informant On a birth or death certificate, the person who provides the information to the REGISTRAR.

Inland Revenue A government board, formed in 1849, to collect various types of taxes.

Inventory A list of someone's personal possessions, made on their death, giving the value of each and the total value of the estate.

Irregular marriage See CLANDESTINE MARRIAGE.

Journeyman A person who is fully qualified to practise a particular craft or trade but is employed by another person. See also APPRENTICE; MASTER.

LDS Latter-day Saints. See the CHURCH OF JESUS CHRIST OF LATTER-DAY SAINTS.

Letters of administration A document granted by a court to those with a claim to the estate of someone who died without leaving a will. Commonly called an ADMON.

LMA London Metropolitan Archives.

Maiden surname A woman's surname before marriage.

Marriage licence A document issued by an ECCLESIASTICAL authority to a couple wishing to marry without the calling of BANNS.

Master A qualified craftsman, tradesman or artisan who employs others. See also APPRENTICE; JOURNEYMAN.

Mormon Church See the CHURCH OF JESUS CHRIST OF LATTER-DAY SAINTS.

The National Archives Formed in 2003 by the amalgamation of the PUBLIC RECORD OFFICE and the HISTORICAL MANUSCRIPTS COMMISSION.

Naturalisation The act of making someone a citizen of the country. Originally the same as DENIZATION, but the term came to imply that citizenship was granted by Parliament.

Nonconformist Any Protestant who does not conform to the doctrines and usages of the established CHURCH OF ENGLAND.

OPR Old Parish Register, referring specifically to Scottish parish registers.

Parish registers Books kept by the Church of England to record the births (baptisms), marriages and deaths (burials) that took place within each parish. The main source for family historians prior to the introduction of CIVIL REGISTRATION in 1837.

PCC Prerogative Court of Canterbury.

PCY Prerogative Court of York.

Peculiar An administrative unit that is outside the normal ECCLESIASTICAL hierarchy.

PR PARISH REGISTER.

PRFD Principal Registry of the Family Division.

Primary sources Documents (such as CERTIFICATES and CENSUS RETURNS) which were created by recognised authorities, such as the Church of England or the state.

PRO Public Record Office (now The National Archives).

Probate calendars Indexes to all wills proved in England and Wales, produced annually from 1858.

Province The senior administrative unit of the CHURCH OF ENGLAND. England is divided into two provinces: Canterbury and York. Until 1920, Wales was part of the province of Canterbury; but since then it has been an independent province, the Church in Wales.

Quakers See SOCIETY OF FRIENDS.

Quarters From 1837 until 1983, the GRO INDEXES for each year were divided into four quarters recording events registered between January and March, April and June, July and September and October and December. The quarters are commonly referred to by the last month.

Registrar A person appointed to register the births and deaths in a specified SUB-DISTRICT. Also responsible for performing civil marriage ceremonies.

Registration district An area established in 1837 as part of the CIVIL REGISTRATION process. England and Wales were divided into over 500 such districts. A Superintendent Registrar was appointed to be responsible for each district.

Relict The widow of a deceased man.

St Catherine's House An office in London, which, between 1973 and 1997, housed the GRO INDEXES.

Society of Friends A religious group founded by George Fox around 1650. Commonly known as QUAKERS.

Society of Genealogists A charity whose objects are to 'promote, encourage and foster the study, science and knowledge of genealogy'. Their library has a large collection of family histories, civil registration and census material, and a wealth of other material of use to family historians.

SoG SOCIETY OF GENEALOGISTS.

Spinster An unmarried woman.

Sub-district A sub-division of a REGISTRATION DISTRICT.

Three Denominations A group that was formed in 1789 to represent the political interests of the Baptist, Congregationalist and Presbyterian denominations.

Tithe maps Maps dating from around 1840, showing individually numbered parcels of land in each of the tithe districts; linked with APPORTIONMENTS.

TNA THE NATIONAL ARCHIVES.

Trade directory A publication listing tradesmen and other residents, by address and occupation, usually within a specific town or county.

Widow A married woman whose husband is deceased.

Widower A married man whose wife is deceased.

Useful addresses

Borthwick Institute of Historical Research
University of York, Heslington, York Y010 5DD
www.york.ac.uk/library/borthwick

British Library
96 Euston Road, London NW1 2DB
www.bl.uk

British Library Newspapers
Colindale Avenue, London NW9 5HE
www.bl.uk

Dr Williams's Library
14 Gordon Square, London WC1H 0AR
www.dwlib.co.uk

Federation of Family History Societies
PO Box 8857, Lutterworth LE17 9BJ
www.ffhs.org.uk

General Register Office
Certificate Services Section, PO Box 2, Southport PR8 2JD
www.gro.gov.uk

Institute of Heraldic and Genealogical Studies (IHGS)
79–82 Northgate, Canterbury CT1 1BA
www.ihgs.ac.uk

London Metropolitan Archives
40 Northampton Road, London EC1R 0HB
www.cityoflondon.gov.uk/lma

The National Archives
Kew, Richmond, Surrey TW9 4DU
www.nationalarchives.gov.uk

Principal Registry of the Family Division
Probate Search Room, First Avenue House, 42–49 High Holborn,
London WC1V 6NP
www.justice.gov.uk/courts/probate

ScotlandsPeople Centre
3 West Register Street, Edinburgh EH1 3 YT
www.scotlandspeoplehub.gov.uk

Society of Genealogists
14 Charterhouse Buildings, Goswell Road, London EC1M 7BA
www.sog.org.uk

Useful websites

Major commercial websites
www.findmypast.co.uk
The biggest UK-based commercial family history website, with access to the GRO indexes to births, marriages and deaths (including the overseas indexes); census returns for England, Wales and Scotland; British Army and Militia service records; Merchant Navy service records; passenger lists (outwards) and much more.

www.ancestry.co.uk
The UK section of Ancestry, giving access to the GRO indexes; census returns for England, Wales and Scotland; British Army service records for the First World War; probate calendars for England and Wales; passenger lists (inwards) and much more.

Other commercial websites
www.thegenealogist.co.uk
www.familyrelatives.com
www.genesreunited.co.uk

Archives and libraries
www.nationalarchives.gov.uk/a2a
The Access to Archives database contains catalogues describing nearly eight million items held in archives throughout England, dating from the 10th century to the present day.

www.nationalarchives.gov.uk/archon
A list of UK repositories giving contact details and providing links to their websites.

www.nationalarchives.gov.uk/documentsonline
The National Archives' digital document delivery service, with access
to the Prerogative Court of Canterbury wills; First World War medal
index cards; Royal Naval service records and much more.

www.britishnewspaperarchive.co.uk
The British Library's digitised newspaper collection.

http://maps.nls.uk
The National Library of Scotland's online map library

Other important websites

www.cwgc.org
The Commonwealth War Graves Commission's website. Access the
'Casualty Database', listing the 1.7 million men and women of the
Commonwealth forces who died during the two World Wars.

www.cyndislist.com
A US-based, categorised and cross-referenced index to resources on the
Internet.

www.ellisisland.org
Search the records of 22 million immigrants, passengers and crew
members who passed through Ellis Island and the Port of New York
between 1892 and 1924.

www.familysearch.org
The Church of Latter-day Saints' website giving access to the
FamilySearch database, with millions of records of births, marriages
and deaths from around the world.

www.freebmd.org.uk
Access to birth, marriage and death indexes for England and Wales.

www.genuki.org.uk
A comprehensive 'virtual reference library' of information of particular
relevance to the UK and Ireland.

www.oldmapsonline.org
An easy-to-use gateway to historical maps in libraries around the world.

www.rootsireland.ie
The website of the Irish Family History Foundation, providing access to over 19 million Irish records.

www.scotlandspeople.gov.uk
An indispensable resource for Scottish family history, providing access to Scottish civil registration records, parish registers, census returns, wills and other useful resources.

www.ukbmd.org.uk
Links to websites offering online indexes to records of UK births, marriages and deaths.

Further reading

Annal, David and Audrey Collins. *Birth, Marriage and Death Records for Family Historians.* Barnsley: Pen & Sword, 2012.

Bevan, Amanda. *Tracing Your Ancestors in The National Archives: The Website and Beyond.* 7th ed. Richmond: The National Archives, 2006.

Christian, Peter. *The Genealogist's Internet: The Essential Guide to Researching Your Family History Online.* 5th ed. London: Bloomsbury Publishing, 2012.

Christian, Peter and David Annal. *Census: The Expert Guide.* Richmond: The National Archives, 2008.

Cock, Randolph and N. A. M. Rodger, eds., *A Guide to the Naval Records in The National Archives of the UK.* London: University of London, Institute of Historical Research, 2008.

Coldham, Peter Wilson. *The Complete Book of Emigrants in Bondage 1614–1775.* Baltimore, USA: Genealogical Publishing Co. Inc., 1988.

Dixon, Barbara. *Birth and Death Certificates: England and Wales 1837 to 1969.* B. Dixon, 1999.

Dixon, Barbara. *Marriage and Certificates in England and Wales.* B. Dixon, 2000.

Durie, Bruce. *Scottish Genealogy.* 2nd ed. Stroud: The History Press, 2009.

Gandy, Michael. *Catholic Missions and Registers,* 6 vols. M. Gandy, 1993.

Gibson, Jeremy and E. Churchill. *Probate Jurisdictions: Where to Look for Wills.* 5th ed. Bury: Federation of Family History Societies, 2002.

Gibson, Jeremy, Elizabeth Hampson and Stuart Raymond. *Marriage Indexes for Family Historians.* 9th ed. Bury: Federation of Family History Societies, 2008.

Gibson, Jeremy and Mervyn Medlycott. *Local Census Listings 1522–1930: Holdings in the British Isles.* 3rd ed. Bury: Federation of Family History Societies,1997.

Gibson, Jeremy Brett Langston and Brenda W. Smith. *Local Newspapers 1750–1920: A Select Location List.* 2nd ed. Bury: Federation of Family History Societies, 2002.

Grannum, Karen and Nigel Taylor. *Wills and Probate Records: A Guide for Family Historians.* 2nd ed. Richmond: The National Archives, 2009.

Grenham, John. *Tracing Your Irish Ancestors.* 4th ed. Dublin: Gill & Macmillan, 2012.

Herber, Mark. *Ancestral Trails: The Complete Guide to British Genealogy and Family History.* 2nd ed. Stroud: The History Press, 2005.

Hey, David. *Journeys in Family History: Exploring Your Past, Finding Your Ancestors.* Richmond: The National Archives, 2004.

Higgs, Edward. *Making Sense of the Census Revisited: Census Records for England and Wales, 1801–1901.* London: University of London, Institute of Historical Research, 2005.

Humphery-Smith, Cecil R. *The Phillimore Atlas and Index of Parish Registers.* 3rd ed. Andover: Phillimore & Co. Ltd., 2003.

Kershaw, Roger. *Migration Records: A Guide for Family Historians.* Richmond: The National Archives, 2009.

Kershaw, Roger and Mark Pearsall. *Immigrants and Aliens: A Guide to Sources on UK Immigration and Citizenship.* Richmond: PRO Publications, 2000.

Nissel, M. *People Count: A History of the General Register Office* (HMSO, 1987).

Pappalardo, Bruno. *Tracing Your Naval Ancestors.* Richmond: The National Archives, 2003.

Spencer, William. *Air Force Records: A Guide for Family Historians.* 2nd ed. Richmond: The National Archives, 2008.

Spencer, William. *Army Records: A Guide for Family Historians.* Richmond: The National Archives, 2008.

Spencer, William. *First World War Army Service Records: A Guide for Family Historians.* 4th ed. Richmond: The National Archives, 2008.

Spencer, William. *Medals: The Researcher's Guide.* Richmond: The National Archives, 2008.

Watts, Christopher T. and Michael Watts, *My Ancestor Was A Merchant Seaman: How Can I Find Out More About Him?* 2nd ed. London: Society of Genealogists, 2004.

Yeo, Geoffrey and Philippa White, eds. *The British Overseas: A Guide to Records of Their Births, Baptisms, Marriages, Deaths and Burials Available in the United Kingdom.* 3rd ed. London: Guildhall Library, 1995.

Index